The Murder of Christine Jessop

Annie Belshaw

Published by Trellis Publishing, 2021.

While every precaution has been taken in the preparation of this book, the publisher assumes no responsibility for errors or omissions, or for damages resulting from the use of the information contained herein.

THE MURDER OF CHRISTINE JESSOP

First edition. July 11, 2021.

ISBN: 979-8224536306

Written by Annie Belshaw.

THE MURDER OF CHRISTINE JESSOP

ANNIE BELSHAW

The Murder of Christine Jessop

Small communities were regarded as safe during the 1980s. Families flocked there from large metropolitan areas in order to live comfortably and away from crime. Queensville was the ideal place for the Jessop family since they had two young children who were still in school. However, one autumn day completely changed their lives. Christine Jessop, a tiny nine-year-old girl vanished from the street while walking back to her home. Unsure of her fate, the community gathered and searched for her, hoping they would find her alive. But as weeks went by, it was clear that something sinister happened to this child. First, they suspected she was kidnapped which provided the family with some hope. However, police were not so certain in that theory.

Once they found Christine's body, police started the investigation which was flawed from the very beginning. They zeroed in on a single suspect, ignoring the other possibilities. In the end, it was determined that the police made a huge mistake, leading to the reopening of the case which stayed that way since 1995. It has been almost thirty-four years since Christine Jessop has been murdered and her family is still searching for the answers. This case divided the Canadian public, who blindly believed in their justice system. The cold case unit is in charge of the case at the moment and hopefully, they will solve it soon because they have the main evidence which is very valuable – the DNA of the killer himself.

Early life

Christine Jessop was born in Queensville, Ontario, Canada on November 29th, 1975. It is a small town just north of Toronto, and it is known for being a small and safe community. Christine lived with her parents Bob and Janet Jessop as well as with her adopted brother Kenny. They were a typical Canadian family at that time where the father had a steady job while the mother stayed at home and took care of the kids. Christine was a small girl, unusually tiny for her age. But that didn't stop her from playing and enjoying sports. She was very active and would run around for an entire day. Her friends would describe her as a little bit of a tomboy.

Christine also loved animals and was very protective of them. She wanted to be a veterinarian, and her parents supported her dreams. Christine had a dog named Freckles, and the two of them were inseparable. She used to bring frogs to her house and keep them as pets. Not to forget that Christine was fearless, especially when a bat suddenly flew into her room. She didn't scream and acted like the animal was just a bird. But even though everything looked alright from the outside, Christine didn't have an easy childhood. It would later be revealed that her adopted brother Kenny, as well as one neighbor, abused Christine when she was young. It is still unclear what kind of consequences it had on Christine's life, but they certainly weren't positive.

The day of the disappearance

October 3rd, 1984 started as a typical day for the Jessop family. The kids were off to school, while Ken went to work. Janet stayed at home in the morning with plans of running some errands in the afternoon. Christine came back home from school at 03:50 PM and she was dropped off by the bus right in front of her home. She picked up the mail from the mailbox and went into her house. The place was empty because her brother was still at school and the parents were out. Christine placed the mail on the dining table and set her school bag on the chair. Sometime around 04:00 PM and 04:30 PM, Christine decided to take a short walk to the grocery store and buy some bubble gum. The man working at the store confirmed that she was inside, but he wasn't sure about the exact time. One neighbor was on the street as well, and he noticed Christine passing by. He was the last person to see Christine alive.

Christine did make plans to meet with a friend from school at the local park. They were supposed to bring their toys and play together. That friend did wait for Christine at the park at 04:30 PM but the girl never showed up. Bob and Janet Jessop arrived home around 04:10 PM. They saw the mail on the table, as well as Christine's school bag but they couldn't find her anywhere in the house which was unusual. After waiting for a couple of minutes, they started phoning her school friends to see if she was at one of their houses. They got a negative answer every single time. Clearly alarmed, Christine's parents started walking through the neighborhood hoping she was playing somewhere. But once again, Christine was nowhere to be found.

The Jessop family was starting to panic, and they contacted the police sometime between 07:00 PM and 08:00 PM. The officers arrived at their home immediately and talked to the parents hoping they would find out more details about where Christine might be. The parents told them they talked to all of Christine's friends and that no one had seen her after school. They also mentioned that Christine was not problematic or had any issues with her family, so the thought of her running away was unimaginable. The law enforcement knew that they might have a missing person case on their hands. They quickly organized a massive search of the area hoping they will find the girl that night or the following day. But there were no results. It seemed like Christine simply disappeared. The police continued to search Queensville regularly, talking to the possible witnesses who might have seen Christine alive but as the time went by, so did the hope they would find Christine alive.

The interviews and the suspect

York Regional Police took the investigation to a whole new level when they started interviewing the neighbors who lived near the Jessop family. They were certain someone had seen something on that day in October. Surely, they pieced together a timeline of Christine's movements on the day of the disappearance, but they also asked everyone if they had seen someone suspicious on that day or if they had any idea who might have been involved in the disappearance. The majority of the interviewed neighbors told the police about their odd neighbor who lived next door to the Jessop family. His name was Guy Paul Morin, and he was twenty-three years old at the time.

When the police asked Christine's parents about Guy Paul Morin, they also confirmed he was a little bit unusual to them, but he rarely interacted with their daughter. However, the police zeroed in on Morin mostly because they had absolutely no other solid leads. What made him the perfect suspect was the fact that he still lived with his parents and that was a bit unusual at the time. Not to forget that he played saxophone and clarinet, was quite well-known in the local music scene and was a member of several bands. He mostly communicated with his bandmates and people with similar interests, usually avoiding his neighbors. Another thing that made Morin stand out was his obsession with bees. He had beehives in his backyard and could spend hours cleaning them as well as taking care of the insects.

Even though he was in a large band, Guy Paul Morin rarely went out to have fun with his friends. He didn't smoke or drink and led a solitary life. This made the entire neighborhood think that he was somehow involved in the disappearance of Christine Jessop. In a way, he did fit their picture of how a kidnapper could look like, and they pointed the finger at him. Another detail that made them think he was behind this crime was Morin's reluctance to join the search for Christine. Instead, he stayed behind his house, tending the bees while other neighbors walked around the houses, trying to find the little girl.

This was enough for the detectives, and they decided to bring Guy Paul Morin for an interview. Morin talked about the things he did on the day Christine disappeared. He worked at Interiors International Limited in Toronto with his parents. The time cards were used back then, and Morin's confirms he left at 03:32 PM. As soon as he got into his car, he drove in the direction of his house, stopping by to purchase the groceries, gas, and other necessities. In the end, he arrived at his house sometime around 05:00 PM and 05:30 PM. His parents and sister were in the house, and Morin's brother-in-law was just leaving. He saw Morin bring in the shopping bags. Morin's mother prepared the dinner while he rested a bit in the living room. The family then ate the meal and started working in their backyard even though it was dark outside. Morin and his father used flashlights. If he headed straight home after the work, the earliest he could arrive in Queensville was 04:15 PM.

The alibi itself was good and detailed, but it needed additional confirmation. The detectives then brought in Morin's parents for an interview hoping they could confirm this information. But while his mother talked to the police, Morin's mood changed. He started staring ahead, never moving his eyes from the wall. A detective who was present while this took place later said that at that moment he knew they had their guy. Taking into the consideration that one of the police dogs that was used during the search clearly indicated that something was in Morin's car which was parked right next to the house, the detectives focused only on him. They searched the car and discovered a fiber which was taken for an analysis. The experts at the Ontario Centre of Forensic Sciences confirmed that it belonged to Christine Jessop. This was the confirmation the police needed, but there was still no Christine or any clues that could reveal where she was.

The discovery of the body

The Jessop family spent Christine's birthday in November all alone, hoping to hear any kind of news about their daughter. Weeks were passing by and the police did have their prime suspect. However, it appeared that the investigation hit the wall because there were no updates. And then on December 31st, 1984, Christine's body was discovered in a field near Sunderland. It was a cold and snowy day as the police combed the area using garden tools to find traces. A patrol car was called by a farmer who saw something suspicious in the woods. The field was around thirty miles away from her home in Queensville, and the trees were everywhere which helped hide her body for a longer period of time. When the rest of the police force arrived, they saw a gruesome scene. Christine's little body was lying on the ground, partially dressed. Her shirt and sweater were still on while the pants and the shoes were placed near her. Her underwear was around her left ankle.

The scene itself features a couple of evidence that could have been used in determining who the killer was, namely a cigarette butt and a milk carton. Also, other physical evidence might have been lost because the police officers who searched the area walked all over the scene without realizing there was a body nearby. Having in mind the location of Christine's body, the investigators suspected she was driven there. Therefore, someone must have picked her up as she was walking home from the store. She was not a girl who would get into a vehicle with a stranger, so it was possible she knew her killer. After all, Christine disappeared in the middle of the day, so if a person tried to grab her, someone would definitely see or hear the struggle.

The body was sent for an autopsy which revealed the severity of the wounds. Christine was first raped then killed by multiple stab wounds. The look of the scene of the crime did feel unorganized, so it was very likely that the murder was not planned in advance. Instead, the killer simply saw Christine and made a decision on the spot. The murder was done in a frenzy according to the depth and the patterns of the injuries which suggests that they were probably in a hurry or scared that they will be caught. The medical examiner did find DNA traces in the form of semen on her underwear.

The DNA technology was not available at the time, so it is good they placed the underwear in an evidence bag and collected a small sample that would be kept in storage. Christine's lifeless body was found in another county so the Durham Regional Police Service was now in charge of the case. The detectives from Durham who took over went to Queensville and talked with the investigators who worked on the missing person case. The York Regional Police told them everything they knew, including who their main suspect was. They also contacted the FBI in hopes of helping them create a profile of the killer. They ended up going public, saying that they had five suspects, but they are certain one of them stands out from the rest. The detectives read the profile of the killer, and it described Morin perfectly.

Guy Paul Morin was stopped by a police car driven by Bernie Fitzpatrick and John Shepard from Durham Police. They brought him in for questioning, and no matter how much he claimed that he was innocent and had a solid alibi, the detectives were hard to convince. They played a game with Morin where they tried to get him to confess. The two detectives brought him in a room that had his fingerprint placed on a wall. Morin was confused when they told him the fingerprint was found on Christine Jessop's clothes and that it matched his perfectly. Morin tried to tell them he had never touched the girl, but the detectives insisted on the confession. The fingerprint was never found on Christine Jessop, instead, it was taken from Morin's clarinet. In the end, he was charged with the murder of Christine Jessop and the Durham Police was very proud of the work they did because they managed to catch a child killer.

The first trial

Guy Paul Morin entered the courthouse for the first time in January of 1986. His defense lawyer was Clayton Ruby who is famous in Canada as a fearless attorney ready to take on the hardest legal challenges. He truly believed his client was innocent and that the police failed to lead the investigation properly. Ruby claimed that the police first picked out Morin from the list of suspects and then started collecting the evidence that could be linked to him. The prosecution had their whole case laid out perfectly. Morin was the strange neighbor everyone pointed their fingers at. He didn't fit in with the rest of the community, and people found him to be strange. They suspected Morin had a difficult day at work and he saw Christine as he was driving back home. He just snapped and offered her a ride which she accepted because she wanted to get home as soon as possible. But instead of driving her home, Morin assaulted the girl and took her body to a remote location in order to cover up what he did.

The fibers that were found in Morin's car were compared to the ones on Christine's red sweater she wore on the day of the kidnapping and murder. According to the forensic experts, they were a perfect match. The prosecution failed to mention that the Morin and Jessop family used the same laundromat and the transfer of fibers is very common in those instances. As a matter of fact, the amount of the fiber found in Morin's vehicle was quite small, and the chances are they got there by accident. The trial went on because two men who were with Morin during his stay in the jail claimed that he confessed to them. Durham Police detectives visited the two in jail and spoke to the snitches, promising a reduced sentence if they testified against Morin. Both men agreed but refused to be recorded on an audio tape. The identity of these witnesses was never revealed, but they testified Morin spoke openly about the murder while he was locked up.

The cigarette butt which was found on the crime scene disappeared from the evidence locker even though Ruby wanted to use it as proof that his client was innocent. Morin was a non-smoker, and the cigarette butt clearly didn't belong to him. When Ruby asked the police about this small piece of evidence, they told him it was removed because they determined it was left there by one of their police officers. However, when Ruby asked the police officer in question what brand of cigarettes he smoked, it was not a match to the butt found near Christine Jessop's body. Clayton Ruby, scared for his client suggested they use an insanity defense which would help him stay out of the jail. However, that tactic was unnecessary at this time. The trial lasted until February 7th, 1986 when the jury found Guy Paul Morin innocent of the crime he was accused of. There was no solid evidence that could confirm he harmed the girl and the fibers which were found in his car were simply not enough. Morin was acquitted, and he was free to walk. However, the prosecution was not satisfied with the result. They appealed, asking for another trial. Of course, the prosecution won, and Guy Paul Morin was once again the main suspect.

The second trial

The prosecution was better prepared for the second trial because they were aware of the mistakes they made the first time. They still faced the lack of physical evidence and had to work with the witnesses from the previous trial, but the lawyers improved their presentation. Winning the jury this time around was the main goal as well as proving that Guy Paul Morin was responsible for Christine Jessop's murder. The forensic expert was once again the main star of the trial where she presented the fibers found in Morin's car for the second time. However, the expert swore that the fibers matched with Christine Jessop's sweater and that there is no chance it was an error. The girl was in Morin's car, and she had the evidence to prove it. Once again, the laundromat detail was not mentioned. The possibility of the fiber transfer was never discussed.

The second trial saw an introduction of an additional physical evidence linking Morin to the crime – a single hair that was found tangled in Christine Jessop's necklace. The forensic expert confirmed that the hair belonged to Guy Paul Morin because it was the same color, type, and length. The sample of Morin's hair was obtained when a policewoman posed as a hairdresser for a band. She got hold of a lock of hair that could be tested. Since they had no actual eyewitnesses to the crime, the prosecution once again called the jailhouse snitches to the stand. The jury took them seriously this time, completely ignoring the fact that the two men were getting benefits from testifying against Morin. They repeated their stories from the previous trial, but this time the jury believed their accounts of Morin confessing to the murder while he was waiting for the first trial.

The lawyers defending Guy Paul Morin claimed that it was physically impossible for him to be in Queensville at the time when Christine Jessop disappeared. They had a timestamp from his place of employment which showed exactly when he left the building. No matter how hard he tried, there was no way he could reach his home on time to kidnap Christine. Ruby who led the defense once again mentioned that the police had more suspects on their list, but they focused their attention on his client because he was different and stood out from the crowd. His alibi was solid but it seemed like the jury believed the prosecution more this time. On July 23rr, 1992 Guy Paul Morin was found guilty for the murder of Christine Jessop. He was sentenced to life in prison which meant there was no way he could be released unless his lawyers manage to file a successful appeal. Having in mind that Morin was accused of killing and raping a little girl, his stay behind the bars was pure hell. The other inmates abused him regularly, but he persisted, hoping that his defense team would find a way to get him out.

The DNA evidence and the aftermath

The DNA technology started being used regularly in criminal cases during the 1990s. Cases all around North America that had DNA samples stored as evidence were tested in order to determine who the perpetrators were. Guy Paul Morin was locked behind the bars at the time, but his defense lawyer Clayton Ruby filed an appeal to the sentencing. Ontario Court of Appeal was looking at this case when the semen found on Christine Jessop's underwear was tested in a laboratory. It was determined that the DNA found on Christine didn't match Guy Paul Morin which meant that an innocent man was accused of the murder and was serving a sentence for something he didn't do. This was more than enough to force the Court of Appeal to speed up the process.

It was January 23rd, 1995 when Morin's appeal was accepted due to the DNA evidence findings. He was acquitted on the spot and set free. Fearing that he might sue the entire justice system, Morin was granted $1.5 million dollars as a compensation for everything he went through. With Morin out of the jail and not on the list of suspect anymore, the public demanded to know what happened with the investigation and why they locked up a wrong man. An inquiry was launched, discovering a lot of interesting details that tell a different story about the physical evidence and how it was analyzed, namely the fibers found in Morin's car. Of course, the jailhouse snitches were closely looked at as well, and the inquiry uncovered they were prepared for the testimony by the detectives from Durham. Plus, they were promised a lesser sentence which was never discussed in the courtroom during any of the two trials.

One detail that came up during the investigation was the alternation of the timeline in order to dispute Morin's alibi. Detectives Fitzpatrick and Shephard approached Christine Jessop's mother and brother, asking them to say they arrived home at 04:35 PM and that they discovered the girl was gone. This could give Morin enough time to get home and kidnap Christine, completely destroying his alibi. In the end, the DNA which was collected from the scene was never matched to anyone in the database. The experts are still testing the evidence on a yearly basis but there are no results.

Christine's mother Janet divorced her husband Bob at the beginning of the 1990s as the pressure from the case ruined their marriage. She still fights for justice and hopes she would live to see the case resolved. On the last anniversary of Christine's death, she said: "I want to find him and that's my goal." Christine's mother is not satisfied with the way the investigation was led and demands answers. That is evident from the statement she made to the local media: "Where is the person that did it? We are talking thirty-two years later. She'd be forty-one or forty-two now. Where is he? That's the question I have. The second question I have is, why?" She apologized to Morin for the change of the statement which eventually landed him in prison. The case of the murder of Christine Jessop is still open and investigated by the police.

CHILD KILLER MAGGIE YOUNG

JAMES FALCON

14

Who was Maggie Young?

Maggie Young's case is relatively unknown today. In fact, even at the time, it did not seem to receive the attention that it perhaps deserved. This was undoubtedly, at least in part, due to the fact that Maggie and her young family lived in Hawaii. News travelled fast around the island, of course, but the mainland didn't pay all that much attention. The story was covered in newspapers across the country, but after the story was first told on page ten or worse, reporters showed little interest. Almost none of them covered the story of what happened after Maggie's arrest.

Moreover, this is a case which took place more than fifty years ago now, in 1965. Believe it or not, this was a time when serial killers, true crime and murder mysteries didn't receive as much attention as they do today. Take, for example, Casey Anthony: she has spawned a decade of public outrage which has seared itself onto America's cultural consciousness. But Maggie Young didn't, not way back in 1965. Hers was just another story.

Just like Casey Anthony- and if anything, exactly like Andrea Yates- Maggie Young killed her own children. She drowned them, one by one in the bathtub, and laid them back out on their beds afterwards... But unlike Yates, Young didn't live out the rest of her life between four padded cell walls. Maggie's life became unbearable after her medical treatment helped her to overcome her delusions, and she realised what she had done to her loving family. She escaped from the oversight of medical staff, took off across the grounds of the facility, and took her own life.

That was the end of the story for almost four decades, until the story of Andrea Yates hit headlines. James Young stepped into the spotlight to help people- and Russell Yates, Andrea's husband- understand what it is like to lose your family to the hands of a loved one, and live with the consequences. Since interrupting his private life to help others overcome post-partum depression and post-partum psychosis, he went quickly back and disappeared from the radar once more. And, since, that has truly been the end of the story.

Maggie's descent into mental illness

The case occurred so long ago now, in a time before the advent of the internet or even cell phones, that finding any published information on Young is actually a difficult task. Before she took her children's lives with her own hands, little to nothing is known about Maggie, her home life, or her former husband James Young. We do know that she was an ash blond, and that her family had moved to Hawaii a generation before. Maggie's mother, Mrs. Chauncey Brown, lived in North Augustus, South Carolina.

Maggie, her husband James and their five children lived on Nalopaka Place, in the suburb of Aiea in Honolulu. The area has a population comparable to a small town, of around 10,000 today but undoubtedly fewer then. The area is North West of the main city, and is actually quite close to Pearl Harbor. Part of the suburb, Aiea Heights, enjoys wonderful views of the bay; Nalopaka Drive is too close to the sea to have any real view at all. Aloha Stadium, home of the University of Hawaii Rainbow Warriors and the largest stadium on any of the islands, is a minute's walk away (although it wasn't opened until 1975).

The couple lived with their five youngest children. Maggie had two adult children, who she had raised in a previous marriage. Counting all of her children, Maggie had six daughters and one son. Her youngest was just eight months old in November 1965, and her eldest with James was an eight year old son. In 1965, their children were Jessica, an eight month old daughter; Jeanette, 2 years old; Judith, 3 years old; Janice, 5 years old, and James Frank Jr., who was 8. Maggie's husband James was an Air Force captain, stationed at Hickam Air Force Base near Honolulu.

What information we do have comes from James Young himself, and a select few news stories from the Honolulu Star-Bulletin. Maggie was born around 1927, which made her 38 years of age when she committed the crimes which gave her a notorious place in history. Prior to her crimes, just like Andrea Yates, Maggie was sent to hospital several times for her mental illness in the years leading up to the last major event of her life.

James Young described the situation in detail, many years later. He wrote that she had very slowly and gradually begun to exhibit signs of depression, which eventually became a completely psychotic state. According to James, she was tired all the time due to her awkward sleeping schedule, which took in all hours of the day; she would even sleep in her clothes.

"Her behavior slowly changed until nothing I nor the children did was right," he wrote. After months of deterioration, Maggie was unable to take care of her youngest children- her children with James. Of course, this being the early 1960's, the fact that Maggie was at least temporarily unable to care for her children was a bigger deal than it would be today. They were not taken into care, but left to Maggie's two eldest children, her two adult daughters. These two daughters did not live at home with their mother, but had long since left and gotten married. They would visit when they could, and juggled care between them.

"After they left, I would come home to find the children in dirty or wet diapers. I would change them, give them their baths and get them ready for bed. During all this she [Maggie] would be in bed," Young wrote. James was an Air Force captain, who flew regular missions and could be gone for days at a time. Perhaps because of his time spent away from home, James found it difficult to recognize that Maggie was suffering from a mental illness of some kind.

As her descent continued, and Maggie did not find the support she needed, she began to have hallucinations and visions. As Maggie and her family were very devout people, these visions were often religious in nature. One night, for instance, she left her family alone and disappeared for over three hours. When she finally came home, she claimed that she had come back from church- having been to marry Jesus Christ. When she talked with her husband about what had happened, she wasn't clear, but she told James that the Virgin Mary was now his grandmother.

Even accounting for her love for her religion, it was clear that Maggie was suffering with debilitating delusions. It was clear that she would be unable to continue playing any role in caring for her children. Not long after her disappearance, she attacked her husband with a broom as he tried to leave for work one morning. She shouted at him: according to James, "she said, 'They are out there. They have come to kill me.'"

Rather than leave his wife, James stayed home that day. He wanted to have his wife committed, for her safety and for his own, and for the safety of their family. Maggie was unpredictable, delusional and beginning to exhibit signs of violence. No matter what the diagnosis would prove to be, she was becoming more of a risk day by day.

But James was pushed back when he called the hospital. He was told that in order for his wife to be committed, she would have to go to the hospital and commit *herself* voluntarily. Quite naturally this seemed like an impossible task at first, but with the help of their priest and their family doctor, James managed to convince Maggie that it was for her own good. She agreed to go- as much as she could have agreed to anything in the state that she was in.

James described what happened next. "She was in the hospital at least a month to six weeks when the psychiatrist told me there was nothing more he could do for her. Any improvement would have to come at home," he wrote in an email to the Star-Bulletin many years later. Again, this was the middle of the 1960's: psychiatric care and medication was not as advanced as it is today, and even now it can be difficult to achieve positive outcomes with a large amount of patients that need mental health care.

"When Maggie was in the hospital, I prayed a lot. Mostly I prayed that she would come home to us. When she did come home, and in a few weeks drowned the children, I blamed the Almighty. Then I realized that my prayers were answered. I should have prayed for her recovery," he wrote. "Then I blamed myself." Maggie had not been ready to come home, but since the medical professionals of the state hospital felt that they could do nothing more for her, she had been sent away anyway; nobody knew precisely what terrible effects that this would have.

The Murders

The murders took place bright and early in the morning. Ed Young was away on another mission, and neither of Maggie's eldest daughters was visiting that day. At 8am, Maggie sent her eldest son to school, and wasted no time in systematically, almost robotically drowning her children. Like Andrea Yates, she drowned them one by one in the bathtub, starting with the eldest and finally killing her youngest last. Her youngest daughter wasn't yet a year old.

Afterwards, she walked to her son's school to bring him home. At 9:30am, he arrived, and Maggie drowned him too. At some point after that, Maggie arranged her children in their beds. When the police arrived later that day, Maggie told the officers that she had been distraught due to her inability to care for her children. She told case investigator John Dickson: "I killed my children". There was no doubt as to what had happened.

She was taken to Honolulu City County Jail, and awaited arraignment on a charge of first degree murder. Even though it was obvious she had killed each of her children in turn, she was only charged with murdering her son, James. Officers charged her within four hours, aware that she was still being treated as an outpatient by the Tripler Army Hospital she had been at from July to September.

A family friend, Mrs. Elaine Marshall of Honolulu, told police that Maggie had called her shortly after the murders. According to Mrs.

Marshall, Maggie asked her about the penalty for murder in Hawaii. Mrs. Marshall said "Oh no, Maggie, what have you done?" to which she replied "I killed them. I killed them all. They were crying. They were crying and I couldn't take care of them all. They were sick and they were crying."

After the call, Mrs. Marshall had immediately contacted the police. Detectives Robert Davidson and Joe Luna rushed to the scene and paid a visit to the family's house, where Davidson asked Maggie: "What seems to be your trouble?" But after a few moments it became obvious what the trouble was. Maggie told them "I killed my children. I drowned them," and the two officers quickly discovered the children, lying in two beds in one of their rooms.

Autopsies done on the bodies over the next few days confirmed that each of them had died by drowning, meaning that in combination with Maggie's many confessions there could be no doubt what had happened- only what punishment should be handed out. Mrs. Marshall told investigators that before she had received Maggie's call that day, she had already been worried that a tragedy might occur because of Maggie's inability to take care of her children.

Another neighbor described Mrs. Young as "very nice", and claimed that the children were good, and always well behaved. Maggie, she said, was always friendly but had appeared more nervous than usual after Jessica was born, the previous December. The family had shown few signs to the outside world that there was a pressure building up; a pressure that would crack and result in the deaths of their five innocent children.

Maggie is committed to the State Hospital

Maggie had spent two months at the Tripler Army Medical Center earlier that year, after her mental breakdown. She was initially held on a charge of first degree murder, but this charge was quickly dropped because of Maggie's obvious delusions. Considering her previous experience with mental illness, court psychiatrists and even the prosecution felt that it would be unfair to try her as if she were in her right mind.

She was charged only with drowning her son, despite having already admitted to killing all of her children. Because she met the criteria of having acted under 'a diseased and deranged condition', she was deemed unfit to stand trial. So rather than be forced to sit in the dock and defend actions she wouldn't even be able to describe, she was immediately sent to the State Hospital, which is still in Kaneohe to this day.

According to hospital administrators, Maggie began to respond to her treatment early on. At this point in time, the Hawaii State Hospital was undergoing radical changes. According to Joanne Lundstrom, a psychiatric social worker working there at the time, the era of 'snake-pit' institutional care for the mentally ill 'was gone, but not too far removed'. During her time there, Lundstrom took part in reorganising the hospital and improving the ways that it cared for patients.

One of the ways in which patient care began to improve was through the use of modern medicines that could help treat psychiatric disorders. Joanne Lundstrom said that they had 'a tremendous impact' when they were introduced, and they were instrumental in helping Maggie Young overcome her delusions and mental illness generally. Today, these kinds of medicines are used to great effect in the treatment of schizophrenia and delusions, just like Maggie had. The only alternative prior to this kind of medication were treatments like electro-shock therapy and frontal lobe lobotomies, which gave less than optimal results.

Unfortunately another hospital administrator, Audrey Mertz, described how Maggie had just begun responding positively to her medication and treatment when the enormity of what she had done began to sink in. It was too much for Maggie. Six months after she was first committed to the hospital, on July 25th 1966, she went AWOL while on a pass to walk around the grounds alone.

She was found soon after, having hung herself from the rafters of a chicken slaughtering shed on the hospital's grounds. It is difficult to imagine the pain she must have felt upon truly understanding what she had done, and finally realising that her children were gone. To lose five children would be a burden that would lead many to a similar end, let alone the burden of living with the guilt if you, as a parent, had ended your own children's lives. Dr. Audrey Mertz spoke to the press after Maggie's suicide, and told them that "the more she improved, the more her realization of her act. She was up against a dead end."

James did not want to speak with press at the time. Although the story was not covered extensively by press on the mainland, the Honolulu Star-Bulletin and other Hawaiian newspapers certainly thought that it would make interesting news for their readers. James Young was, and always has been, a private the delusions Maggie had for what had happened. He couldn't bring himself to blame his wife, even though he had lost his children.

'In her mind she had removed the children from a cruel world and had sent them to a far better place to be with God. I think that the proof that she truly believed this is demonstrated in the fact that as her treatment slowly returned her to reality, she began to realize that what she had done was terribly wrong and eventually she could no longer live with the terrible truth.'

James leaves Hawaii, and reaches out to the press

James Young left Hawaii shortly after the deaths of his children at the hands of his wife. He moved back to the mainland, to California, and allowed the case to be forgotten by history: by all accounts, he is an intensely private man who would rather leave that sad period of his life behind him. That, of course, is completely understandable. Since he left Hawaii, he remarried, although he did not have children again.

But when Andrea Yates killed her children in 2001, suddenly, the media began to draw parallels between the two cases. Of course, they shared many similarities- right down to the way that the poor children were killed. Specifically, Honolulu Star-Bulletin reporter Treena Shapiro wrote an article for the newspaper which brought the old case to light. In that report, she quoted an email interview which she conducted with James Young, who she had asked for quotes on how it must feel to lose your family to the hands of a loved one.

James, who had not sought out the media and had not been sought out in turn, was helpful. He was 72 years of age when Yates' story became national news, and perhaps enough time had passed that he seemed happier to talk with the press. He wrote that he hoped that in finally speaking out about the tragedy that had befallen his family, he could encourage others to get help for post-partum depression. He had reached out to the Star-Bulletin by email.

"Since I am the father of those Aiea children, I feel compelled to do what I can to help this woman who is a victim of postpartum depression and the terrible feeling of inadequacy she must have felt—the same feelings my late wife must have felt. Behavior signs we all recognized in hindsight," Young wrote in his first email. "Medical science needs to recognize this condition earlier and help the mother before it develops into paranoid schizophrenia, as it did in the case of Maggie."

"This ill woman does not need to be sentenced to prison; certainly not charged with first-degree murder," he continued. "My wife was charged with first-degree murder. But Hawaii justice recognized her illness and gave her the medical help she needed. Unfortunately she did not survive the cure." Considering that the cure had helped Maggie to realise what she had done, it would perhaps have been kinder to allow her to remain delusional and to never understand the gravity of the crime she had committed.

In a message to Yates' husband, James wrote "[a]ll I can say to him is there is no 'closure' but there is life after tragedy." Young told the newspaper that he managed to survive his ordeal through relying on the support of his family, friends and co-workers. "We need to recognize postpartum depression with psychosis earlier and successfully treat it," he wrote. "We must do whatever we can to prevent another mother killing her children."

Russell Yates reaches out to James

Even though the story only appeared in the Hawaiian press and on the Star-Bulletin's website, Andrea Yates' husband found it and reached out to the newspaper to try and get in touch with James. Although Russell Yates was not allowed to speak out about *anything* related to his wife's case because of a court order, he told Treena Shapiro that he had reached to James and the two had been able to connect over their shared sorrows. The two had spoken over the telephone. "He was encouraging to me and supportive of my wife and me," Yates told Shapiro.

In another email interview with the Star-Bulletin after the two had first spoken, Young wrote that "[a] tragedy resulting from this illness must not occur again. There must be better awareness of the seriousness of this illness." He was, of course, writing about post-partum depression. Young told Shapiro that he had tried to support Yates. Andrea Yates had been on suicide watch since the murders, and was at the time facing the prospect of the death penalty.

According to Shapiro, writing in the Star-Tribune, "Young said he told Yates to keep his faith, not to be ashamed to cry and to be prepared to cope with the pain for the rest of his life. There is no such thing as closure, he said." Considering that Young was 72 at the time that he wrote to Yates, there could be little else that would as accurately convey the horror of what happened that Young still felt no closure after all those years. "I still cry and had my share of tears following his tragedy," Young wrote to Shapiro. "After all these years the tears come less frequently but I have days and nights."

"Christmas is also very difficult. Memories come flowing back. Christmas is for the children. Without them, Christmas is not the same," he continued. Young and Yates shared memories of their kids, which Young told him to cherish. After remarrying, James chose not to have any more children, a decision which his new wife supported. "After I remarried, my wife was understanding and comforting," he wrote.

He also connected with Yates over the way that people take their families for granted, and that before you know it, they could be gone. "I told him that for years, I would experience anger every time I saw someone humiliating a child in public, especially in restaurants. I wanted to tell the abusing parent that they should enjoy their children," Young wrote. "Their time together may be shorter than they think."

James followed the Yates' case in the press, and was disappointed with the guilty verdict that she initially received. Young again wrote to Shapiro, and told her that he had been driving home from work at the time he had heard the news. "To say I was disappointed is a great understatement," he wrote. "I have been following the Houston Chronicle coverage of the trial on a daily basis, and based on the coverage I have read, I could not believe a jury would find her guilty. Even the prosecution's expert witness had left the door open for an insanity verdict."

He had previously written to Shapiro, and had then too talked about the horrible effects of post-partum depression and psychosis, and how important it was that the symptoms of these conditions were recognised and treated as soon as possible. 'I don't mean to say that all parents who kill their kids are innocent by reason of insanity. But those suffering from SERIOUS (postpartum depression) do not need to be in jail. They need to be given treatment,' he wrote. 'Hopefully, the treatment will come before the tragedy.'

Young was a Texas native before having moved to Hawaii for the Air Force, and his children are buried at the Fort Sam Houston National Cemetery. As such, it was no surprise that he felt so strongly about the Yates case. He wrote that he was ashamed of "the Wild West 'hang 'em high' mentality—especially in the Houston courts." "Under the circumstances, I am pleased. ... At least she will receive treatment. I can't help but feel sorry for her and Rusty," he wrote.

Since the Yates case, Young went back to the solitude of the life he had built after the terrible events that tore apart his first family. He was 72 going on 73 at the time, and since the Yates case was over fifteen years ago now, that would be another fifteen years added to his already long life. Although what happened to his young family is not well known, even despite the comparisons that were made between that and what happened to Russell Yates, it's certain that any reader who encounters his sad story could only wish him happiness in this life, or the next.

CHILD KILLER ANDREA YATES

JAIME FOSTER

Andrea Yates

Andrea Yates was, and still is, a devoutly religious woman. She did, and still does also suffer from severe depression and could justifiably be called 'insane'. In fact, that's what she's been called by the courts-for having murdered her young family, one by one, in one of the most shocking criminal cases in recent American history.

Her crime was drowning each of her five children over the course of just one hour, before laying them down in bed as if to sleep. She was initially found guilty of murder, but her charge was changed at her retrial to innocent by reason of insanity. She was then committed to North Texas State Hospital, a high-security facility, and finally to a low security state mental hospital where she remains to this day.

The reason why Andrea chose to kill her children stemmed from her insanity, but expressed itself through her religion. Andrea had always been devout, but had been inspired by her religion and her delusions that her children had been inhabited by demons. It was this that had led her to kill her children on that fateful day.

Andrea Yates' background

Andrea was born July 2nd, 1964, and lived in Houston, Texas during her childhood. She was the youngest sibling from a total of five, and born to Irish and German immigrants. Her friends say that she has suffered from depression since at least her late teenage years, although there were no signs of what would happen because of her mental illness later in life.

By all accounts, she was successful at school, and graduated as class valedictorian from Milby High School 35 years ago, in 1982. She quickly found a job through a two year long nursing program, and went on to work at a University of Texas cancer center for eight years, until 1994. It was during this time that Andrea met Rusty, her husband to be; they met when they were both 25 years old, and living in the same apartment block. Rusty would later recount how they met to the judge and jury, and say how he had no idea how the woman he had met that day could have become the woman in front of him then.

Andrea and Rusty were quickly married, and just as quickly decided to have as many children as God would allow. By 1999, the couple had just had their fourth child, Luke. Their others were named Noah, John, Paul and Luke. A year later, they would have their first girl- Mary. But far from enjoying their blessings, as most families would, Rusty began to notice that Andrea had become depressed.

From 1999 until the murders, which took place in 2001, Andrea showed signs of severe postpartum depression and dreadful delusions. One day in June 1999, Rusty came home to find that his wife had attempted suicide by an overdose of pills. He had come home just in time, and took her to the hospital, where she was prescribed a course of anti-depressants. But this was just the beginning of a downward spiral.

Not long afterwards, Andrea threatened suicide again- this time holding a knife to her own neck, and begging her husband to let her die. Rusty once more took her to the hospital, where she was prescribed the anti-psychotic medication Haldol. She did appear to be getting better for a while, and the family moved to their first house (they had previously been living in a small motor home).

But just a month after her first episode, Andrea suffered a complete breakdown. This time, she attempted suicide twice, whereupon she was finally diagnosed with postpartum psychosis by her psychiatrist, Dr. Eileen Starbranch. Starbranch appeared in court after the murders, and testified that she had encouraged the couple not to have any more children since it would effectively guarantee similar psychotic episodes in the future; but the pair did not want to listen, and conceived their final child (Mary) just seven weeks after Andrea was discharged from hospital.

Because of the birth of her new child, Andrea stopped taking her medication. But she nevertheless seemed stable- at least, until the death of her father in March, 2001. It was at this point that she began to truly circle the drain. She stopped feeding Mary, began to self-harm and spent the majority of each day reading the Bible and doing little else. It got to the point where she required hospitalization, but upon her release it seemed that nothing could rouse her from her psychotic state.

It was then that Andrea first began to seriously consider killing her own children. In May, she drew a bath- just like she would a month later- with the intent of killing them. She even confessed this to her husband Rusty, who of course took her back to her doctor, Dr. Mohammed Saeed; but Dr. Saeed concluded that she had drawn the bath to drown herself, and didn't take Rusty's concerns seriously. Of course, it was on June 20th of that year that she committed her terrible crime.

The killings

From the outside, the family seemed to have been blessed with their children, and seemed happy too. Neither Andrea nor Rusty let on to their friends and neighbors that they were having any difficulties at all. Their children were always neat and well dressed, Rusty worked a steady career job, Andrea was a capable homemaker and home-schooler. But this image was shattered on June 20th, 2001.

According to Andrea herself, in statements she gave to police, she drowned her children one by one in their family bathtub. She stated that she started with her younger sons first, since they were less likely to put up any fight; she then began to drown her daughter, just six months old, when her eldest walked in and asked- 'What's wrong with Mary?'

When her eldest, Noah, realised what his mother was doing, he ran. He tried to escape from the family home, but didn't get far, as Andrea chased and caught him. He was then drowned too, while Mary's body was still floating next to him in the bathtub. It is hard to imagine anything more horrific.

It was Andrea that called the police, saying that she needed an officer right away- although she wouldn't say why. When the police officers did arrive, she immediately confessed: 'I just killed my kids'. Noah was still in the bathtub, and the other three were arranged in their beds as if they were sleeping, Mary in the arms of one of her brothers.

Officers found the family dog tied up in the backyard. Rusty later said that when he had left that morning- which was a matter of minutes before Andrea drew a bath to drown her children- the dog had been outside, but not tied up. During the trial it was claimed that Andrea had consciously stopped the dog from being able to do anything about her plans. But whatever the case, she was taken into custody for what seemed like an open and shut charge- of having murdered her children.

Yates was held at Harris County Jail and was placed on suicide watch. At this point, prosecutors were unsure as to whether they wanted to pursue the death penalty or not, or whether they would be successful if they did; although that being said, Harris County is well known for its administration of the death penalty, since they have put a grand total of 62 people to death since 1977. For context, that would place it third compared to a list of entire *states*, behind only Texas (of which Harris County is a part) and Virginia.

While the prosecution were deliberating, the defense was already certain that they would plead not guilty, on the grounds of Andrea's psychosis. George Parnham, Yates' attorney for her defense, claimed that for a month after her arrest it was impossible to talk to Yates at all due to her inability to interact rationally with anybody, even her partner Rusty.

The Trial

Yates' case depended on a specific Texas law. In Texas, for a defendant to plead the defense of insanity, they have to be able to prove that they could not tell the difference between right and wrong (at least, at the point in time when the crime was committed). This is perhaps the most stringent check on the use of the insanity defense anywhere in the United States.

This law meant that even though Yates' lawyers could bring up her repeated suicide attempts and her repeated psychiatric hospitalization, these facts actually weren't enough for a successful defense on their own. No matter how ill, and no matter how delusional Yates may have been, if the prosecution could prove that Yates knew what she had been doing was wrong then the courts would have no choice but to sentence her as they would a person in their right mind.

Because of the importance of this element to the case, the prosecution decided to bring in perhaps the most famous psychiatrist practicing today, and no stranger to court cases like these, Dr. Park Dietz. Dietz should be well known to anybody who follows these sorts of cases: he gave testimony in the trials of the Unabomber, Susan Smith (who also killed her children through drowning) and John Hinckley, the would-be assassin of Ronald Reagan.

Most famously, Dietz worked on the case of Jeffrey Dahmer, when he successfully convinced the court to find him legally sane. If anybody could convince the jury to convict Andrea as a sane women, the prosecution thought, it would be Dietz. His testimony lasted two days, and was the media highlight of the trial. He gave a Powerpoint presentation to clarify the reasons why, he argued, Andrea should be found guilty as she was legally sane at the time.

During his testimony, the courts showed recorded footage of interviews that Dietz conducted with Andrea. "Before you did it, did you think it was wrong?" Dietz asked.

"No," Andrea replied.

"Why did you not think it wrong?"

Andrea answered, "If I didn't do it, they would be tormented by Satan."

It almost seems backwards: Andrea's legal sanity was proven by her delusions. But for the courts of Texas, this proved to be enough. In March, 2002, the jury had little choice but to find her guilty of murder due to the fact that she was legally sane at the time of the crimes according to Texas law, rightly or wrongly. The prosecution had been intent on seeking the death penalty, but the jury rejected the option. She was, instead, sentenced to life in prison with a chance of parole after 40 years. In effect, Andrea was guaranteed to be in prison for almost the entirety of her adult life.

Appeal and retrial

Even though the case for Andrea's guilt was unassailable, the defense nonetheless managed to order a retrial based on a charge of false testimony, levelled against Dr. Dietz. The defense claimed that Dr. Dietz had either lied or made a mistake during his testimony, with regards to an episode of Law & Order which he claimed could have inspired Andrea's actions. The only problem was that no such episode, which Dr. Dietz had claimed bore remarkable similarities to the story of Andrea's crimes, had been aired.

"Shocked at the possibility of having made a factual error, even one unrelated to Mrs. Yates, I immediately researched the issue, with help from the writers and producers of 'Law & Order,' and within hours determined that my recollection was probably incorrect," Dietz wrote in a statement explaining what had happened. An author, and one-time writer for *Law & Order* Suzanne O'Malley reported to the press that no such episode as Dietz had described had ever been aired.

O'Malley spoke to CBS News' *The Early Show* that Yates could now understand what she had done, but had nonetheless (in her opinion, based on letters she had received from her) been legally 'insane' at the time of the crimes. "She understands what happened. It's a living nightmare for her. I don't think she'll ever forgive herself. She asks her husband, Rusty Yates, how he forgives her. And he said, 'Andrea, if I were in a car driving the five children and I had a heart attack and had a wreck and they all died, would you blame me? Would it be my fault?' and she said, 'No.' He said, 'That's the same thing with you. You're mentally ill. It's a brain sickness.'"

In fairness to Dietz, he had written to the prosecution long before the retrial, in a letter dated March 2002. He admitted in the letter that he had made a mistake, possibly confusing two different episodes with one another, and thus given incorrect testimony during the trial. These two episodes were on Susan Smith and a young girl who had killed her baby after it was born instead of admitting that she had been pregnant. Both of these episodes were shown in the weeks leading up to Andrea's murder of her children. The letter that Dietz wrote to prosecutors was never brought to the attention of the trial. Once the information came out, however, the appellate court found that a retrial would be necessary because of the profound influence that Dietz had had on the outcome of the original trial.

The focus of the retrial was once again on Andrea's mental health and the actions of those around her that may have exacerbated her illness. At the trial, Rusty admitted to having left Andrea alone, despite it being recommended no to. He said that he and the rest of her family hoped that it would give her greater independence and confidence, and eventually help her to fulfil her role as a mother. But she still showed signs of mental difficulties throughout this time, for instance when she tried feeding Mary solid food, choking her, when she was still far too young.

Some of Andrea's family were supportive of the idea, but others, not so much. Her brother Brian Kennedy appeared on Larry King after the trial to recall that Rusty had told him he hoped that leaving her alone would give Andrea a 'swift kick in the pants', and motivate her to improve her own life. Andrea's psychiatrist, Dr. Starbranch, also expressed her dismay at the pair's plans to try to improve Andrea's mental health. In particular, during a visit just prior to her being discharged as a patient, the couple told Dr. Starbanch that they planned on having more children despite her opposition to the idea.

At the trial, Rusty claimed that he had not known the effects that these actions would have in the long run. 'If I'd known she was psychotic, we'd never have even considered having more kids,' he told the press during the trial. He also expressed his regret at not having seen the signs of her illness appearing sooner.

Without the influence of Dietz's testimony, Yates was this time found not guilty by reason of insanity. The trial concluded on July 26th, 2006 whereupon Andrea was moved to the North Texas State Hospital, Vernon Campus. Shortly afterwards, she was transferred again, this time to Kerrville State Hospital, a low-security facility in Texas.

Difference of opinion

Rusty had been under a gag order for the entirety of the trial, meaning that he couldn't speak out about his nerves before the verdict. After leaving court it became clear that he had been waiting for this moment for a long time: he told reporters, "It's a miracle." But the prosecution were far from happy with the verdict: "Five years ago, Andrea Yates called police to inform them of what she had done to her five children," prosecutor Joe Owmby told the same group of reporters. "It was no mystery then who ended their lives. We are extremely disappointed with the verdict." The second prosecutor working with Owmby added, "This case has always been about bringing justice for these children," and they felt that justice had not been served in quashing Andrea's sentence.

But Rusty demanded, "Who are they really serving? Do they think the children want Andrea to be in prison? Do they think we, her family on either side, want Andrea to be in prison? Is it of any public benefit for Andrea to be in prison? Is she a danger to anyone?" "It's amazing to me," He went on. "I'm so proud of the jury for seeing past that."

In their explanation for reversing Andrea's conviction, the Court of Appeals judges stated that "there is a reasonable likelihood that Dr. Dietz's false testimony could have affected the judgment of the jury." But Dietz argued the point after the end of the trial: "In short, I made an honest mistake and took immediate action to correct it," he said. "I am angry that a false accusation by a defense lawyer has been so widely promulgated in the press."

The Vice-President of the APA (American Psychiatric Association) spoke extensively to the press in the aftermath of the retrial, expressing her support for the decision. "It is a great relief to hear that justice has prevailed," APA Vice President Nada Stotland, M.D. told Pyshciatric News.

" It's heartbreaking that she was convicted in the first place. It was clear that some people were swayed by their intense feelings about the sanctity of motherhood," she said. "They could not accept any excuse for a mother harming her children. So they thought it was essential that the court send a message that would convince other mothers out there that they couldn't get away with harming their children.

"Others could not grasp the possibility that a person could carry out effective plans and activities while psychotic or on the basis of psychotic beliefs. This is a recurring confusion in cases involving a psychotic defendant.

"There is also a persistent sense that society is too lenient overall, a belief that criminals are claiming insanity far more often than is the case and still far more often than this defense actually prevails. Many people simply don't believe in psychiatric conditions as genuine diseases. They feel that the punishment of those who break the rules is essential to the maintenance of a just society."

That being said, Andrea remained in prison. The fact of her mental illness had not changed, whether she was judged to have been legally sane at the time of the crimes or not. At the very least, she would now be able to receive better treatment for her afflictions than she had in prison- something that both she, and her family, was happy for.

Was it her anti-depressants that were to blame?

Andrea's family, friends and neighbors firmly believe that the anti-depressants she was administered were to blame for her psychotic mental breakdown. According to Suzy Spencer's book about Andrea,

Breaking Point, she was taking 450 mg of Effexor daily, until the final few days before her breakdown, when the amount was drastically reduced by Dr. Saeed. Rusty claimed that he protested to the doctor, since his own research had told him that dramatic reductions in intake of Effexor can have terrible side effects. Nevertheless, Dr. Saeed insisted on lowering the dose.

Dr. Saeed argued that Andrea was already taking far too much of the drug, and that the risks of continuing to take it in such large amounts were greater than the risk of reducing the amount by roughly a third. Homicidal ideation is one of the accepted side-effects of the drug, and Andrea had been taking far too much- twice the recommended dose- for two months prior to the murders. At the trial, Dr. Lucy Puryear gave testimony as an expert witness. She claimed that Dr. Saeed's actions were normal medical practice, and that he could not be held accountable on this front for Andrea's psychotic break. Rather, she claimed, it was the fact that Andrea was taken off her regular dose of Haldol which was to blame.

What about religious influences?

An alternative theory is that Andrea's religious influences were a major cause of the tragedy that occurred. Not long before the event, Rusty met a preacher named Michael Woroniecki: Woroniecki was, and is, well known for his fire and brimstone sermons on the topic of Hell, and for his regular newsletter on the topic of Hell and the Rapture entitled *The Perilous Times*. It was around the time that Rusty met Woroniecki that Andrea's delusions took on the extra dimensions of demonic or satanic possession, prophecy, and references to the end times.

After the trial, ABC Primetime's Chris Cuomo claimed on air: "[Andrea Yates'] delusions were fueled by the extreme religious beliefs of a bizarre, itinerant street preacher named Michael Woroniecki..." He believed that Woroniecki's preaching and writings had inspired Andrea to believe that the end times were coming, and that the devil was at work in her community- and through her children. Woroniecki, of course, denied the accusations. He claimed that he had not been close to the family, a sentiment echoed by Rusty himself.

That being said, it was clear that at some level Andrea's delusions drew upon the ideas of her deeply held religious views. In conversations with her prison psychiatrist, Andrea has since stated that she had long considered killing her children. "It was the seventh deadly sin. My children weren't righteous. They stumbled because I was evil. The way I was raising them, they could never be saved. They were doomed to perish in the fires of hell." Andrea's attorney agreed: "Bottom line [is] she thought she was saving their souls," Parnham told ABC News.

Andrea Yates today

Andrea Yates is, of course, still imprisoned. She is still held at a small mental health facility, Kerrville State Hospital, and will turn 53 this year. Sources close to Yates have told newspapers that she still watches home videos of her young family. Of all the inmates at this particular facility, Yates is the only one not allowed outside. She requested just a two hour pass for permission to go to a nearby church, but this was refused.

Yates herself has refused to talk to the press, but her defense attorney George Parnham has confirmed that she will almost certainly remain at the same facility from now until her death. He has also given a small window into Andrea's life at the hospital, and described his relationship with her. "Long ago, I crossed the professional line," Parnham said. "I treat her as if she were a child of mine."

Describing her everyday life, he said "...There are no wires. There are no fences [at Kerrville]. She wears makeup, wears blue jeans, she wears earrings when she wants to," Parnham said. "She devises little arts and crafts and sells them anonymously at trade shows." Any money she makes is given to the Yates Children Memorial Fund, which was founded by her attorney and his wife Mary. The proceeds go towards women struggling with mental health issues. Despite the changes in her life, Parnham has confirmed that Andrea has few visitors who take the time to see her.

Describing the charity and the effects that it has, Parnham has said "...It turns a tragedy into a positive force. It means a lot to prevent other tragedies in many ways. Now we talk with attorneys about mental health. People always ask me about Andrea in a very compassionate way. That's a far cry from the position the state took years ago, when they sought the death penalty."

Rusty has been asked by the press whether he forgives his wife. "Yes... Forgiveness kind of implies that I have ever really blamed her. In some sense I've never really blamed her because I've always blamed her illness." It has been well over a decade, now, since he and his wife lost their children due to Andrea's mental illness; but no matter the facts of the case, it remains difficult to imagine or sympathise with how Rusty can have forgiven his wife. Most people would not have the strength.

CHILD KILLER MANLING WILLIAMS

40

CRYSTAL STONE

Manling Williams was born in 1979 as Manling Tsang. She tended to go by the nickname "Ling" while growing up. As a child, she was diagnosed with various learning disabilities and experienced many challenges academically while in school. Williams was the result of an unwanted pregnancy between her two parents, and she was nearly aborted. Ultimately, she was born into a family that didn't want her, and they treated her as such throughout her childhood with copious amounts of verbal and physical abuse.

In her childhood, Williams struggled to make friends. At one point when she was growing up, she stole money from her parents in order to buy friends at school, as she couldn't make them no matter how hard she tried. She did not do well socially. That incident resulted in a public scolding that was so severe and inappropriate that Child Protective Services became involved. While her mother was chastising her in front of her peers, she slapped her face repeatedly. Although Child Protective Services was called, nothing tangible came of it, and the case was closed. Manling remained with her parents and her sister for the remainder of her childhood and into her early adulthood.

Many would later testify that Manling's parents repeatedly called her stupid due to her lack of success in school, and that physical abuse went on as well. In one incident, a foreign exchange student who was living with the family recalled that her father slapped her face four or five times when she was suspected of stealing money from a friend. Manling ran to her room in tears.

In 1999, Neal Williams met and fell in love with his 20-year-old coworker at Subway, Manling. "He thought she was beautiful," Neal's mom, Jan Williams, later said in a statement to reporters. "He liked that he could talk to her about a lot of things." Neal was considered to be affable and intelligent. He was well-liked, and liked to watch Star Wars and quote Monty Python. He was considered to be very bright and was particularly close with his mom, Jan, and his older sister, Mala.

Shortly after they began dating, Manling became illegitimately pregnant with Neal's child. On July 26, 2000, Neal and Manling's had a baby boy, whom they named Devon. Devon was described by his grandmother Jan as silly, sociable, and tolerant. He wished to study monkeys when he grew up and attend Whittier College, which is where his grandmother worked. Everyone loved Devon. A family friend had chosen to have him as the ring bearer in her wedding. "He couldn't stand to see someone upset or treated unfairly," the friend recalled. If he saw someone being treated unfairly, or if he saw that someone felt sad or was upset, he took steps to fix it, even at a young age.

Jan Williams recalled one painful memory of Devon having some normal anxiety about nighttime and being afraid of the dark, a memory which stings his grandmother to this day. The two were singing a nighttime song about a dragon. Devon expressed concern because the song alluded to little boys who died in their beds. "I told him he was safe in his bed, and he wasn't," his grandmother later said sadly.

In 2001, Manling and baby Devon were in the car with Judy, Neal's mom. Manling officially asked Judy for permission to marry his son. "Only if you promise not to hurt him," she replied lightly, and the pair laughed, having no idea of knowing what lay ahead.

Having had a child out of wedlock did nothing to improve Williams' ongoing tumultuous relationship with her parents. She was forced to move out of their home and temporarily lived with friends and her mother-in-law, Jan Williams. Neal and Manling eventually became engaged, got married at a courthouse, and later had a big wedding at a Taiwanese church. The trio then moved into a condo in Rowling Heights in Los Angeles county, California, where they would live until everything ended. The neighborhood was cozy and safe, and the neighbors were friendly.

Manling and Neal's second son, Ian, was born in the Fall of 2003. Ian liked to pester his older brother, and "threw himself into life with great abandon," according to his grandmother's recollections. He would do things like get his head stuck between the railings on the banister, build a ladder out of chairs and climb to the top, and knock down whatever structure Devon had just created. He also hated any sort of nickname or pet name, and insisted vehemently, "My name is IAN!"

A few years went by where, by all appearances, Manling, Neal, Devon, and Ian were a happy and regular family. At this time, Williams worked at Marie Callender's as a waitress, while Neal did a lot of computer work from home. In the months leading up to the incident, Manling had connected with an old friend named John Gregory via MySpace, and subsequently began an affair with him. This was a man that she had had an attraction, or rather an infatuation, for since the days of high school. Almost immediately after their affair began, Gregory began to pressure Manling to get a divorce and ended up breaking things off with her shortly after, while promising that they could get back together if she ended up terminating her marriage. Meanwhile, Williams had grown tired of being a mother and a wife, and was feeling very distant from her children.

Beginning in June of 2007, Manling began to randomly tell her friends that she was having dreams of Neal smothering their sons and then killing himself. No one made much of these comments, aside from thinking that they were disturbing and unfortunate. Williams and her husband had been having significant marital problems, often resulting in profanity-laced arguments and slamming doors that could be heard by neighbors outside of their home. The home they lived in was filled with piles of clothes and trash, with unwashed dishes and more trash on the kitchen counters, and was chronically very unkempt. However, despite their marital difficulties, Neal was by all accounts an excellent father. He enjoyed reading to his children, playing catch with them, and taking them to baseball games.

On August 7, 2007, Maling smothered her two young sons with a pillow in their bunk bed, and slashed her husband to death with a sword in the family's condominium. With regard to her children, Ian was in the bottom bunk with a teddy bear blanket, and Devon was in the top bunk, under a Spongebob blanket. Her husband Neal was 27 years old at the time, the same age as Manling. Devon was age seven, and Ian, age three. Autopsy results would show that the boys had died within two hours after eating their last meal, which was pineapple pizza delivered to the home at 8:20 pm. Computer records showed that after she smothered them, Manling left the boys dead in their beds and checked her boyfriend's MySpace page. She then went out with friends to dinner to TGIFridays. A friend who was at dinner with her would later testify that Williams was behaving normally, and that Williams often spoke lovingly of her children. Four days prior to the killings, on August 3, Williams had sent her lover a single red rose, with the message "thinking of you." She had signed it as being from a secret admirer.

Neal was asleep in bed when Mailing returned home. Manling retrieved and used a katana sword that had been given to Neal by his mother, as he was a sword collector. The knife had a 10-inch handle, a 20-inch blade, and was incredibly sharp. While he was sleeping, she stabbed him in the chest. Neal did not die in the bed, which indicated that he had gotten up tried to run in an attempt to escape.

The autopsy report would show that Neal's hands were mangled as he tried to fend off the attack, and he had a giant "X" slashed on his torso. He lost the tips of two fingers and broke several other fingers attempting to defend himself. He had 22 wounds on his hands alone. He only made it as far as the top of the stairs, which was a short distance from their bedroom, and the katana was found near his body. Neal was stabbed and slashed 97 times total in the attack. In his final moments, he begged Williams for help, a call which was left unheeded. He suffered a fatal wound when he was initially stabbed through the heart, damaging his right ventricle and his aorta, which takes blood to the brain. This was actually the first strike from the katana, but it wasn't an immediately fatal one. Autopsy results showed that both of his lungs were punctured and filled with blood (500 cubic centimeters in the right lung, and 200 cubic centimeters in the left). In addition, he suffered a wound through his back that went "through and through" and departed his body via his neck, damaging his thyroid gland in the process. One of the other most damaging wounds went through his small intestine. In addition, a "chopping" type of wound was located on the back of his neck that fractured his skull and caused bleeding in the brain. Neal's mother would end up having chronic, recurrent nightmares of his nearly severed hands after learning about them in trial. Deputy Tim Bryant later testified that he nearly fell when he stepped over Neal, because there was so much blood that had saturated the carpet around him.

Immediately following the murder, Manling typed a fake suicide note on Neal's behalf stating that Neal had killed the children and then himself. The letter stated that Neal was having an affair and hinted at killing the children before committing suicide. "Please for give [sic] me for being a coward and not being there for you," Manling wrote under the guise of Neal's voice. She posted the note on MySpace. She disposed of all bloody clothing in a dumpster a fair distance from their home. These clothes were later recovered and were confirmed to have Neal's blood on them. Then she returned home and ran outside, screaming to neighbors at 7:30 am that someone had killed her family.

Several neighbors ran to assist and after speaking to Manling, went into the house before the police arrived, not understanding what they would find. In court, one neighbor would describe seeing Neal at the top of the stairs. "I seen Neal laying there, stabbed up. I looked into his eyes and blood was just dripping and dripping." This same neighbor found the little boys and described through tears what he found while on the stand. "I shook the little blanket but there was no movement, nothing, no movement."

Manling's account of what had happened became contradictory almost immediately. Upon calling her neighbors over at 7:30 am via her frantic screaming, she told them she had gone out for Red Bull and cigarettes and had returned to find the crime scene. She then told investigators that she had gone for a drive because she couldn't sleep, then later stated that she had gone grocery shopping (though she was wearing boxer shorts, smelled of alcohol, and was barefoot when her neighbors saw her, suggesting that she hadn't recently gone anywhere).

When Neal's mother, Jan Williams, heard the news, she got a ride to the sheriff's station right away, where she met with Manling's parents. The trio hugged and cried as they waited for more news. They waited for Manling to come out after her interview with police. However, Manling was never released, and soon, a terrible realizations began to set in.

For several hours, while being interviewed by investigators following the discovery of the bodies, Manling feigned sadness, grief and bewilderment on camera. She said things like, "Does anyone know if my husband is okay? I want my babies. Please let them be okay." Only after investigators found a bloody cigarette box in her car and confronted her did Williams confess to the crimes. Blood was found in a spot on her bra that matched where Neal's blood was found on the bloody shirt that was thrown into the dumpster. Neal's blood was also found on her feet. After her confession, she was arrested on three counts of homicide one day after the murders, on August 8, 2007.

Detective Donald Walls recalled that Manling was arrogant in her interviews, that she was relaxed as if they were having a normal lunchtime conversation, and that she made jokes about the TV show CSI. The Williams' neighbors in the 18200 block of Camino Bello in Rowland Heights, California, were first shocked and then horrified as police spread crime scene tape around their property and began carrying out multiple bins of evidence. One piece of evidence that was later shown in court was a dictionary that had a page marked by having a knife placed inside. On this page was the definition of the word "marriage." In the yard lay discarded equipment: a football, a bat, and a plastic pitching machine.

Manling originally stated in her confession that Neil had "passed out drunk" the night of the killings, but toxicology reports later showed that he did not have drugs or alcohol in his system. He was sober when he died. After Manling's arrest, it took more than a year for the first preliminary hearing to take place due to repeated delays and postponements. This process was very hard on the victim's family. Neal's mother and sister were particularly open with reporters throughout the process as they waited for the trial process to begin.

With the verdict in, the next part of the legal process was the penalty phase, in which jurors would recommend whether Manling should receive life in prison or the death penalty as her sentence. Manling's defense attorneys, Tom Althaus and Haydeh Takasugi, argued that Manling should receive a life sentence and not the death penalty, arguing that the murders were not calculated, but rather "a sudden mistake," and that Manling was in a state of "extreme emotional and mental disturbance" when the killings occurred. They noted that "it was clear that the family unit was unraveling." However, as Los Angeles County Deputy District Attorneys Stacy Okun-Wiese and Pak Kouch pointed out, Williams had put on latex gloves prior to killing her husband, indicating that the killing could not be correctly defined as "spur of the moment." The defense attempted to paint Manling as a socially awkward loner who was mentally unstable and who was overburdened by cultural expectations.

The defense also argued that Williams had a difficult upbringing, and that her life was defined by pain, heartbreak, and "diminished dreams." They noted that she was reputed to be a very charitable person prior to the killings, that she was previously well known for lovin her husband and children (a contradictory assertion to several neighborhood eyewitnesses), and that she had no history of violence. A few additional witnesses continued to contradict this picture, however, such as one of her neighbors, who indicated that Manling rarely said more than hello, and that "she would just stand outside her house, smoking and smoking." The defense focused almost solely on the upbringing and abuse Williams experienced at the hands of her mother. Manling's father, Kai Tai Tsang, while on the stand, appealed directly to Neal's mother and apologized. "I feel really sorry. Please forgive me. As a father, I didn't do good. That is why it happened. I am sorry."

Williams' former lover, John Gregory, testified that after Manling contacted him on MySpace in June of 2007, the two went to dinner with two other people from their high school, during which time Manling discussed that she wasn't happy at home or in her relationship. In July of 2007, Manling went to see Gregory in Santa Barbara for a weekend, and the two had an affair. According to his testimony, Gregory ended the affair a few days later. He reported that Manling seemed "normal" throughout the affair and also upon breaking up. Gregory had initially denied the affair to investigators, but later came clean. "I felt really uncomfortable and slightly responsible that I contributed to her emotional state," he said. Manling's friend Melaney Ramirez also testified with regard to Williams' emotional state, saying that according to previous conversations they had had, Manling felt forced into marriage because she accidentally became pregnant. Another friend, Jaclyn Bailey, testified that Manling and Neal would fight "almost every day," and that the fights would often escalate to screaming. Bailey also stated that she had lived with the Williams for three months, and that she was "beyond shocked" because she always thought Williams loved her children, even if there were struggles in the marriage.

With regard to whether or not the killings were premeditated, testimony during Williams' trial indicated that the suffocation method of using a pillow by which she killed her first child took five to 10 minutes, which was ample time for Williams to consider her actions. However, she then went on to kill her second child in precisely the same way. This in additional to wearing the latex gloves and mentioning the manner of death to friends up to two months prior to the killings, made it difficult for the defense to form a solid argument about the killings being spur of the moment.

Neal's mother was present during the trial and was often seen taking notes on what was being presented in an almost clinical manner. However, one week into the trial, she broke down as blood spatter pictures were being shown to the jury, and she saw one of her grandson's favorite stuffed animals (a dragon that her grandsons had named Puff) in the background of the photo. She was also forced to watch a clip of Manling calmly telling a detective what Neal's last words were ("Help me").

Mangling went to trial in November of 2010, and the trial took approximately six weeks. A jury, after deliberating for eight hours, convicted Manling of three counts of first-degree murder, along with the special allegations of using weapons and lying in wait. The jury of six men and six women was unable to agree, with a vote of 8-4, on whether life in prison or the death penalty was a more appropriate punishment, so the decision was given to a second jury. The second jury recommended in 2011 that Williams be put to death.

There was much controversy around the sequence of the two juries who were tasked with deciding the outcome for Williams. Manling's sister, Shun Ling Tsang, urged the judge to consider life without parole instead of the death penalty rather than retrying the penalty phase after the first hung jury. She had given testimony during the trial that her sister's behavior had changed in the months leading up to the murders, and that she would often call her sister in the middle of the night "just to talk," which was new and unusual behavior. She argued that the prosecution's continued pursuit of the death penalty was "ego driven" and "politically motivated." After the first jury was unable to come to a decision, members of both families asserted that they would prefer to see a life sentence with no possibility of parole, and no possibility of appeal. The defense again appealed for life in prison over the death penalty, emphasizing Manling's lack of previous violence, as well as her difficult upbringing. However, the prosecution decided to re-try the penalty phase, which resulted in the death penalty. The second penalty phase of the trial began on April 18, 2011. Prosecuting attorney Stacy Okun-Wiese scoffed at the defense's attempt to pin the murders on Manling's childhood, stating "When did it become okay in our society to commit three heinous crimes, kill your children and your husband, and blame it on your mom?"

Williams was sentenced to death on January 8, 2012 for the murders of her family per the jury's recommendation. "It is the order of the court that you should suffer the penalty of death," Judge Robert Martinez said to Manling. She was 32 years old at the time of her sentencing. Manling, dressed in an orange prison jumper with glasses on, sat in handcuffs and stared down at the table during the duration of the sentencing, then sobbed and visibly shook after the support was read. She leaned on her defense attorney, Haydeh Takasugi, who openly cared about Williams on a personal level, and who was deeply invested in the case. Manling was often seen in court that way - head down, eyes down, unable to look the world in the face.

Neal's mother, Jan Williams, expressed gratitude that the trial was finally over, citing the "terrible" impact the events had had on everyone involved, including the Tsang family. She has stated "This is their tragedy, too. I don't blame them for anything." It had been very difficult for her to attend as many hearings and trial events as she had over the past four years, but she made herself go until resolution of the case.

She felt that it was her responsibility to be present at every court date because someone had to be there to "represent the victims."

Pomona Superior Court Judge Robert Martinez stated "The evidence is compelling that the defendant, for selfish reasons, murdered her own two children." He called her desire to start a new life with another man "narcissistic, selfish, and adolescent." He noted that Williams had many family members who would have willingly taken the boys in, and that their deaths were abhorrently unnecessary. He remarked that each of the three killings was deliberate and premeditated without question. Lastly, he remarked that he was not in the position to forgive, as "the ones in the position to forgive are not with us."

There is some question as to whether or not Williams will actually ever undergo execution. California is known for delaying executions for those on death row indefinitely. There are over 700 people who have been sentenced to death in California. However, only 13 people have put to death in California since 1976, none of whom have been the other 19 women who are already on death row in California. Neal's mother took some comfort in the resolution of the case. "The legal process will no doubt go on for probably the rest of my lifetime. But I feel like I am leaving something behind today. Something is finished," she told reporters.

One of the most notable things about Manling has been her silence. She has essentially gone radio silent since her incarceration. She has reportedly become involved with the church services within the prison where she resides, and the leader of this church testified in court that she had come to know Manling well and that she didn't feel she was "evil." It was also shared in court that many of the children who knew Devon and Ian became very traumatized upon learning of their deaths, and even more so when they learned that they were killed by their own mother.

Jan Williams maintains a blog to this day that is open to the public and started almost immediately after the death, detailing her memories, events, and coping with regard to what happened to her family. It's called Grief's Journey, and provides a raw and rare insight into the life of a survivor of a murder victim. She also keeps a fairly public Facebook page, which shows a morbid and personal look into her experience over the course of the trial. In a post from 2010, Jan writes, "In planning a suicide, it might be well to remember that it is very difficult to stab yourself repeatedly in the back, especially when your hands and fingers have been severed. That's free advice."

CHILD KILLER PAULINE ZILE

CRYSTAL DENNIS

Pauline Zile was born June 13, 1970 as Pauline Yingling. Some reports assert that her mother, Paula Yingling, abandoned Pauline in her childhood. However, her mother was a visible presence later in Pauline's life and the two now appear to be close. Pauline's father, conversely, is little more than a question mark. Pauline's only sibling, Matt Yingling, grew up to be a firefighter and emergency technician, and John Yingling, their only other known immediate relative, is Pauline's maternal grandfather. The two were not close, and John was very removed from the events of her life.

While many facets of Pauline's early childhood remain unknown, we do know that she had a difficult adolescence. When Pauline would undergo a murder trial for the death of her daughter as a young adult, her defense team was notably silent on her upbringing and provided few, if any, facts about who she was or where she came from.

We do know that as a teenager and then as a young adult, Pauline moved from one ramshackle apartment to the next, and had little in the way of education. She became pregnant while dating a teenage boy named Frank Holt in 10th grade at age 16, and subsequently dropped out of high school.

This pregnancy resulted in marriage, and their child, Christina Diane Holt, was born five months later on May 23, 1987. Being a married teenage mother proved to be too difficult for Pauline, and the marriage resulted in divorce not long after it began, one year later. Frank Holt filed for divorce on June 14, 1988, and initially expressed interest in gaining custody of Christina, as he stated that Pauline was an unfit mother who was also a flight risk. Around this time, she began taking part in a series of jobs in different restaurants. According to Maryland court records, she also struggled with drug and alcohol issues, as did Christina's father. Christina never lived with her father in her short life.

Pregnancy would remain a major theme of Pauline's teenage and early adulthood years. By the age of 24, she had become pregnant and borne children three additional times. However, Pauline gave her first child Christina up willingly as she was only 17 when Christina was born, and her marriage had failed. "It was a case of babies trying to raise babies," her mother later said to a newspaper in an interview.

Christina went to live with her paternal step-great-grandmother, Dorothy Money, as neither parent showed any serious interest in permanent custody and both continued to struggle with drugs and alcohol. Christina would live with Dorothy from the age of five months to five years. They lived in a comfortable, middle-class neighborhood in Maryland. Christina was reported by friends and neighbors as a sweet girl who was very outgoing. Money reported that Pauline would come up from her residence in Florida to see Christina once per year, but also stated that their visits were short, and that neither Christina nor her mother seemed to feel very comfortable or enjoy their visits very much, particularly in Christina's younger years. When Christina was five, Dorothy signed guardianship over to her adopted daughter, Judy Holt, who lived a block and a half away. Dorothy struggled with severe arthritis and was 70 years old. Christina would still come to spend weekends with her, and Dorothy kept her room with her pink canopy bed just the way it was in anticipation of her visits.

Judy Holt kept Christina for 22 months, but eventually decided that she did not wish to raise Christina long-term, and felt that Christina should be raised by her mother. By all accounts, Christina was very excited to live in Florida with her mother, and to meet the two little half-brothers that she had heard of but never seen. It has been reported that Judy Holt drove Christina to Florida with little to no notice to Pauline and left her in her care. It was this lack of notice that was likely the first in a series of events that led to Christina's death. Dorothy Money later reported that Judy had taken Christina to Florida without her knowledge, and she was so upset about this fact that she severed the relationship with her adopted daughter. Dorothy did not know Pauline's phone number, and she never spoke to Christina or Pauline again.

When Christina was two years old, Pauline met and married John Zile at age 19, who had moved to Florida in 1987, violating his probation. She quickly bore him two sons, and stated later that John forced her to get an abortion for an additional pregnancy. When Christina was unexpectedly left in their care, she was seven months pregnant with an additional baby that she would later give up for adoption due to financial issues. When Zile went back to Maryland to face charges that he had violated his probation, Pauline wrote a letter to the judge pleading for his release, and describing how she was having difficulty paying rent without him, even while working two jobs. In the letter, she described him as a "terrific guy."

John Zile had a troubled youth. Records show that he spent part of his youth incarcerated on unspecified charges in three different involuntary youth shelters and one group home. He had a ninth-grade education and had once been suspended for "being rowdy," according to school records from 1986. In 1984, he was found guilty of burglary, as he had broken into a home and stolen a rifle and some silverware. He was given a five-year sentence, broke probation twice, and served several additional months as a result. He was described as having drug and alcohol problems and bouncing among odd jobs (such as painting cars, working in restaurants, and installing drywall) and lived in a series of different residences throughout his life.

Pauline continued to lead a difficult existence with her husband and children, often having to live in pay-by-the-week motel rooms in order to get by. Neighbors reported that she was at one time going door-to-door and selling children's videotapes in order to obtain gas money. A former landlord of the Ziles stated, "I felt sorry for them. I don't know why. Her eyes always looked sad, truthfully. I just thought maybe it was from working all the time and being with the kids when she was off work; she never had time for herself." The same landlord also reported that Pauline worked hard while John drifted from job to job, staying inside all day, blasting music late at night, and often quitting his short-term jobs without notice.

One neighbor said Pauline and John's two young boys were often spotted in the windowsills of their apartment, banging on the windows and waving at anyone who passed. They would continue this behavior until their father saw them and pulled them away from the windows. The Ziles would not allow management into their apartment for cleaning or repairs. Neighbors reported that Pauline didn't even let the children out to play, and they would forego invitations to birthday parties and playdates. The Ziles worked a succession of restaurant jobs after meeting one another, often together (he as a cook, and she as a waitress). Their landlord later reported that Pauline and the children rarely left the apartment, and that John always answered the door, and he always delivered the rent money.

The landlord who managed the complex had a son who noted that that conditions in the residence were horrible. "It was dirty. When you'd walk by the room and the door was open, there was stuff all over the floor. The kids' room was really dirty and it smelled. There were clothes everywhere, food on the tables, potato chips and shoes, toys, glasses, paper cups and stuff."

Sometimes after work, Pauline would want to get a drink with her coworkers. However, one of these colleagues later reported that John would call her and tell her to get home and take care of the kids. One neighbor reported that Pauline and John didn't get along well, and that she would often go days at a time without hearing from him. Prior to her sudden and expected arrival, Pauline spoke fondly of Christina to these colleagues. She would show them pictures, talked about how well she was doing in school, and talked about how they would exchange packages and cards through the mail. Pauline also stated to her neighbor, Donna Dunn, that she left Christina in

Maryland because she couldn't afford to give her a good life, but that she hoped they would be reunited and live together someday.

After having lived with relatives in Maryland for most of her live, she moved in with her mother, her stepfather, and her two younger half-brothers in a one-bedroom apartment in Riviera Beach. Four months later, she was dead. It wasn't long after her unexpected arrival that the abuse at the hands of her stepfather began. At one point, John beat Christina in a bedroom in front of a family friend named Chad Brannon. He picked her up by the shirt, threw her on the bed, beat her repeatedly with a belt, and then pulled down her pants and showed Chad the welts caused by the injuries, according to information provided by Chad during testimony.

Christina was kept out of school in the weeks leading up to her murder in order to hide her frequent injuries. She had only attended school for a total of five out of 22 days that year. Her murder took place on September 16, 1994. Christina was in second grade. She was three feet, nine inches tall, and weighed 44 pounds. Her death occurred around midnight. She was beaten to death by her stepfather, John Zile, while Pauline stood by and watched, failing to intervene. Christina was beaten until she collapsed and went into convulsions, and was found to have ultimately died by suffocation as she choked on her own blood and vomit. John Zile had held his hand over her mouth and also stuffed a towel in her mouth during the beating to muffle the sound of her screams and cries. John Zile later admitted that the girl was beaten after repeatedly soiling herself and defecating on the floor, but called the death an accident.

The Ziles' former next-door neighbor, Dayle Ackerman, testified that she had overheard the murder. She was getting dressed when she heard a man say "Why did you shit on the floor in front of me?" The neighbor then heard the sounds of the shouting, crying, and hitting. She later testified that heard the man hitting the screaming child over and over until the child fell silent. She did not do anything to assist the child or to intervene. Ackerman testified that she then heard a female voice say, "John, that's enough." In her final moments, Ackerman did not hear Christina calling for her mother. Prior to the fatal beating, neighbors reported that they heard John cursing at and slapping the girl on multiple occasions. After the beating, John Zile reported that he tried to revive Christina via CPR and by dunking her in a tub of cold water, but it was too late.

Pauline was eight months pregnant at the time, and ended up having her fourth child from prison shortly thereafter, who was given up for adoption immediately afterward. Three days later, she went to Christina's elementary school and withdrew her, but did not ask for any school records. This was unusual as school records are often required for enrollment in another school. As they days and weeks went by, Pauline tried to hide the death by telling school officials that Christina had returned to her home in Maryland. She pawned her daughter's bicycle and videotapes, and used that money to purchase the shovel and tarp to bury her daughter. John buried a five and a half foot grave, then threw that shovel over a bridge.

Four weeks after Christina's death, Pauline went on television to plead tearfully for the return of her daughter, suggesting that she had been kidnapped from the restroom of a flea market in Fort Lauderdale called the Swap Shop. During this television appearance, Pauline pleaded for her return, but also kept referring to Christina in the past tense ("She was a nice girl"). She also led authorities to her car, where she had planted a half-empty bottle of juice and a half-eaten bag of candy on the car seat. She concocted a story about how she and Christina had planned to spend the day at the beach. Pauline described specific details about her fictional trip to the Swap Shop with Christina, stating that Christina was excited about seeing the circus and going on the amusement rides.

As a result of Pauline's appearance on television, Christina's photo was plastered across local and state news media, which prompted a frantic search and also generated a lot of public interest and concern in this particular case. Over 10,000 flyers were posted throughout southern Florida by the Adam Walsh Center, who became involved in the case. The Ziles and Christina's biological father taped separate interviews about the case for America's Most Wanted. This public interest and concern carried would carry over into the subsequent trials of her parents.

Police became suspicious soon after Pauline's missing child report. There were no witnesses that reported ever seeing Christina at the Swap Shop. Authorities discovered that she had been withdrawn from school several weeks earlier, but not placed in a new one. They also discovered that no one had seen Christina alive in quite some time. They obtained a search warrant and examined the Zile's residence. Blood was found throughout the apartment, including on a pair of Christina's jeans, her bed, the walls, and the floor. Traces were also found in the couple's car and on some knives in a toolbox that was in the trunk. The couple had kept Christina's body wrapped in blankets and sheets in a closet for several days before burying her. She was buried in a vacant lot near a shopping center in Tequesta, Florida. In the separate trials for both parents, the coroner would report that Christina had bruises on her left eyebrow, left lower jaw, left cheek ,and right cheek. Bruises were also found on both arms, her right leg, her right knee, her thigh, and on her buttocks. There was a deep cut inside her mouth that occurred due to the blunt force trauma she experienced.

John's boss later commented that he worked side-by-side with John in the days following her murder. "I saw no signs of emotion, no signs of stress. It just blows my mind," he stated. The woman who lived next door to the Ziles, Linda Kauppinen, said that the knowledge of Christina's death haunted her daily. "Every time I closed my eyes, I saw her in that closet." The back of Linda's closet touched the back of the Ziles' closet where Christina was temporarily kept. "I just kept getting that picture."

Pauline's two youngest children told investigators that John beat Christina's buttocks, that Pauline and John did not like Christina, and that Christina was dead. During the early stages of the investigation, the Ziles continued to arouse suspicion by halfheartedly fleeing from authorities and not showing up for requested appointments with police. In one instance, Christina was reported found (which was obviously an error). Pauline did not rush to see the child, which investigators found to be odd. The Ziles spent some time during the investigation staying with Pauline's mother. In late October 1994, as the investigation grew more heated, the couple tried and failed at a double-suicide in an orange grove. They had planned to asphyxiate themselves in their white Cadillac. Eventually, after failing a lie detector test and being interrogated for several hours, Pauline came clean and implicated her husband in the killing in exchange for limited immunity. After hearing that his wife had made a statement, John decided to "come clean," to "do the right thing," and he led authorities to Christina's grave.

One wonders how much Paula Yingling knew about Christina's case, given some of the oddly specific quotes she gave in the early days of the search for Christina, who was initially considered missing. "We're just very, very upset and are hoping for her safe return. From what I'm told, police don't think anyone in the family had anything to do with this,"

After John's arrest, authorities worked to determine if they had cause to charge Pauline as well, given that she had limited immunity for the statement she had made to police. During this time, she continued to stay at her mother's beach house, where she received frequent death threats from the public.

Eventually Pauline was charged with first-degree murder, a charge that matched John's. Both were potentially eligible for the death penalty. Prior to her trial, Pauline released a statement through her attorney, saying "I pray that everyone who ever knew and will know me will forgive me for not being a strong person and eventually will trust me again. I will never forget seeing Christina on the living room floor nor her laying on the bed."

During Pauline's trial, it was noted by many that a primary goal of the defense was to make Pauline look as youthful and innocent as possible by dressing her in all pastels, and making her look like little more than a child herself. This wasn't a difficult task, as the brown-haired, blue-eyed woman in her early twenties stood at a little over five foot three. The defense team, which was a well-known father-son attorney duo, argued that Pauline was dominated by her husband, and that she was both helpless and powerless to stop the beatings against Christina. They even asserted that she was "as much a victim as Christina herself." A friend of Christina's described her on the stand as a "weak female," and said it was difficult for her to go against the grain, even if it included or resulted in the death of her daughter.

A witness from The Swap Shop said he saw Pauline rehearsing her television appearance, and was doing what she could in that rehearsal to appear frantic. Neither Pauline nor Christina showed up on the security tapes at the Swap Shop.

Ninety minutes after closing arguments, Pauline was found guilty of first-degree murder and was sentenced to life in prison without possibility of parole on June 7, 1995. She was 24 years old. She was also convicted of three counts of aggravated child abuse, each carrying a sentence of 13 years, to be served concurrently with her life sentence. Upon being sentenced, Pauline remarked, "At least I can sleep tonight," through tears as she was ushered away. As part of the sentencing, she was also forced to give up her remaining two children (Chad, age three, and Daniel, age five at the time). The two boys were adopted together by an unknown family. Pauline has stated that the family does keep her updated on their lives.

The judge remarked that the evidence showed that Pauline was unhappy when Judy Holt brought Christina to live with her, and that she viewed Christina as an unnecessary expense. He also acknowledged that this incident was the first time she had technically been charged with a crime, despite her previous drug and alcohol issues, and noted that he saw her risk as a future danger to society as minimal. This was his rationale as to why she was sentenced to life in prison rather than given the death penalty.

In May of 1994, John Zile's first trial began and ended in a mistrial because the jury was deadlocked. 11 of the jurors felt the charge of first degree murder was an adequate punishment, but one lone juror disagreed, held out for second-degree murder, and would not budge. The second trial had to be dismissed because the judge decided that a court clerk's comments had contaminated potential jurors. The third trial, however, reached its conclusion without incident.

In December of 1996, John Zile was sentenced to life in prison without the possibility of parole for Christina's murder. He also received an additional 30 year sentence for being found guilty on three counts of aggravated child abuse. The defense argued that John never meant to kill Christina, and that his actions after her death "shouldn't be considered."

In October of 1999, the Florida Supreme Court dismissed an appeal Pauline had filed that argued that the statement she gave to police to implicate her husband ended up being used against her as well, and violated her constitutional rights. Six years after Christina's murder, Pauline gave her first interview from the maximum-security prison where she is still held. She described a "pain that's always there," and said she often thinks about what she should or could have done in retrospect. She also stated that she still loves John Zile, though she's not "in love" with him. She argued that she isn't guilty of murder, and said her defense team's representation was grossly inadequate and resulted in the loss of the case. "I don't deserve to be here," she said. "I know I did wrong, but I don't think it's right for me to sit here for the rest of my life for a crime I didn't commit."

Pauline has learned to express her wants and needs in prison, according to jail records. She has requested a mirror to maintain her appearance, a roommate to assuage loneliness, and has also sought education to obtain her high school diploma. She specifically requested to room with Clover Boykin, a notorious woman accused of killing her five-month-old baby, as well as a nine-month-old baby that she had babysat. In a letter written to jail officials, she wrote, "The protective custody lockdown for my own safety does not affect me. It's the long, lonely days and nights I don't like." Pauline was separated from other inmates, who considered mothers who murdered (or took part in murdering) their children to be "the snake's belly" of the prison population and they were targets for acts of violence. Other inmates also wrote letters and started petitions stating that Zile was receiving special treatment, and that certain deputies "treated her like a celebrity."

During this time, she also filed an additional motion in Palm Beach Circuit Court to have her conviction overturned, and was representing herself.

The Zile case set a number of legal precedents. Her conviction of first degree murder due to failure to protect her child was the first of its type in the nation. She was also the first woman to be sentenced to first-degree murder following a new Florida state law that removed the possibility of parole for those who were found guilty of this crime.

There was much public interest in this case, and the area where Christina's grave was marked was a shrine of sorts for quite some time, with a large cross, notes to Christina, and a variety of stuffed animals left by wellwishers and those who wished that something could have been done to save Christina before it was too late.

It has been noted that gender played a role in this case, specifically with differential application of the criminal law codes. Around the time of Christina's death, a little boy in Florida who was living with his father and stepmother was killed by his stepmother after repeated abuse. Unlike Pauline Zile, a first degree murder charge was not brought against the father for "failing to protect his child," and he was "allowed to get on with his life after the tragedy of losing his son." Some critics have argued that Pauline received a harsher sentence because she is female and the parenting standards and expectations are not applied in a uniform way.

Pauline Zile is now 46 years old. The public still doesn't really know who she is. Two pictures have been painted of her: One is that of an irresponsible and manipulative woman, who chose her husband over her child, and who coldly faked a missing child story for police and television cameras. The other picture is that of an insecure and weak woman, a high school dropout, who once pleaded with a judge to release the man she loved. In all likelihood, she is a combination of the two. Whoever she is, she will remain in prison for the remainder of her days. We may never know her true feelings regarding the death of her daughter, or whether she ever did feel any genuine regret or remorse for what happened to Christina.

KILLER BABYSITTER : THE TRUE STORY OF CHRISTINE FALLING

66

DIANE ULLMER

It is said that cats have nine lives, most understand this as a mildly clever metaphor for the preternatural ability of felines to land on their feet.

The mentally challenged Christine Falling took this saying quite literally, so much so that during her formative years she would regularly take cats up to the top of the highest buildings in her Perry, Florida neighborhood and dropped them off over the roof.

Sometimes she would strangle them instead.

Most of the people that came in contact with her would walk away shaking their head in disbelief at her ignorance.

Stupidity would prove to be dangerous, however, as Christine would seek employment as a babysitter.

Tragically, she would soon graduate from killing cats to killing children.

Christine Laverne Slaughter was born on the 12th of March in 1963 to a poor and dysfunctional working class family in Florida. From an early age it was clear that she had a great deal of cards stacked against her, which included a large appetite, frontal lobe epilepsy (for which she had to take regular and powerful medication to prevent an epileptic attack or seizure) and an astonishingly low IQ.

Still, no one would notice the little girl walking down the street cradling different cats.

"She killed the cats," forensic psychologist Paula Orange said. "Because she wanted to take her rage out on something. Anything. Any small animal would do. She wanted to have power over life and death over something as she didn't have any power in her own life."

Both of her parents were poor and they would fight often. Some were petty outbursts while others turned violent. When these altercations turned physical, and they often did, the police would be called, time after time, typically with little repercussions.

Her father would also sexually abuse her in addition to administering daily beatings when she didn't please him.

"The loss of innocence came early for Christine," Orange said. "Her father was a sick pervert, pulling her into the bedroom as she was watching cartoons."

One day, after one of the daughter and father's incestuous meetings, Christine's father became suddenly irate and began to beat her with a bottle. Her mother rushed her to the hospital where she told an investigating officer that Christine had been in a car accident.

"A car done run her over," Christine's mother said. "I didn't get the license plate."

The physician that examined the little girl felt otherwise. The injuries were clearly caused by blunt force trauma but the police did not follow up.

"Christine and her sister were under the radar of child protective services," Orange said. "And they remained that way for a long, long time. The child protective service was not set up the way now. Christine was savaged as a young child. Like so many victims of sexual abuse, her wiring would change and she would be destined to some kind of tragic life, taking people along for the ride."

According to Christine sister, Carol, their parents were so aloof and detached from the rearing of their children that on one trip to the local supermarket, their mother, Ann Slaughter, simply decided to abandon them there. Shortly thereafter both girls were adopted by Dolly and Jesse Falling (thus adopting the last name over Slaughter). Dolly Falling always dreamed of having children but, due to physiological complications was completely incapable of doing so – for her, the sight of the Slaughter children was a godsend. Jesse Falling knew the Slaughters well and also readily accepted them into his home. However, this newest sanctuary was anything but, for not only did Christine's mental issues cause a lot of problems but there were also rumors that Jesse Falling would regularly sexually abuse the children.

These allegations were investigated and Jesse was twice arrested for allegedly sexually assaulting Carol. The allegations were never proven, however, and he served no jail time.

At the age of nine, both Christine and her sister Carol were taken from the Fallings. They were taken to a child care center located in Orlando following the intervention of a local pastor who worried about the two girls.

The Fallings hesitated with the request but eventually gave in to the advice of the pastor. Their new was called The Great Oaks Village of Orlando, a home for neglected and downtrodden children. Christine liked her new home despite making everyone around her feel awkward. She would often give her fellow children "strange looks" and walk the halls with a vacant gaze.

Christine also developed a habit of bursting out into sudden fits of rage that seemed wholly unprovoked, distressing the other children and caretakers. She was also extremely antisocial and would often move off to sit by herself, hardly ever conversing with any of the other residents of her new home.

"Her rage came about whenever she couldn't deal with something," Orange said. "Like a child crying over a broken toy or spilled milk. The problem was Christine was older now and still exhibiting child-like behavior."

At the age of only fourteen, Christine would marry a twenty-three-year-old man at the behest of her parents. The union was anything but a happy one, often devolving into heated shouting matches and violence.

Christine did not hold back during their physical altercations and on one occasion hurled a thirty-pound stereo at her beau's head.

They would separate only six weeks of wedded "bliss."

After the break-up, Christine would psychologically deteriorate even further. During this period of manic distress, Christine visited the hospital over fifty times yet the physician would never find anything wrong with her.

Nothing except hypochondria.

And yet, time after time, Christine continued to return to the hospital, every time with new and increasingly bizarre and outlandish symptoms.

ADULTHOOD

Christine grew into an oversized Baby Huey looking character as she grew old. She had a bulbous forehead and a child-like way of talking. Uneducated, she applied for jobs in restaurants and schools but was rejected. She held some menial jobs but could not last long in conventional employment.

Her epilepsy, child-like mannerisms and below average intelligence disqualified her from just about every line of work. Luckily, she was well liked by her neighbors, who saw in her an affable childish innocence, and she quickly found herself regularly assuming the role of babysitter for the community.

She had seemingly finally found her niche, gaining a reputation among the community as a caring and reliable babysitter.

"Her smile was disarming," Orange said. "Her demeanor was disarming. No one would suspect her of anything. In fact, she looked like someone who needed babysitting herself."

But on February 25th, 1980, everything changed.

Christine was asked to look after a playful child named Cassidy Johnson, a neighbor's kid.

Cassidy's parents left their child in the care of Christine without any trepidation. The child seemed to like Christine and they looked like they could get along.

A few hours later, however, Cassidy fell ill and was rushed to the doctor.

The initial diagnosis was that the child was suffering from encephalitis, the severe inflammation of the brain which is typically a condition brought on by very serious cerebral infections. The child languished in feverish oblivion for three terrifying days before dying.

The coroner's examination would reveal something else, however. The cause of the brain swelling was blunt force trauma to the girl's skull.

Only one person could have been responsible.

Christine Falling.

INTERROGATION

Christine tried to lie her way through the police questioning. She told them that the child had fallen from the crib and hit her head on the floor.

The police were not in the slightest convinced by there was no evidence to be had and no one else to corroborate or contest Falling's tale. The doctor who had attended to the child was suspicious himself and wrote a letter describing his misgivings to the cops.

His letter was lost and the case soon became forgotten...

MOVING TIME

Christine was smart enough to realize that she should not stick around. She moved to Lakeland, Florida which was becoming a bustling business center.

Christine settled in, finding a place to live in a trailer park where she would spend her days watching television and milling around outside her trailer, smoking and greeting passersby.

She returned to do the only work she knew; babysitting.

Finding work with the unsuspecting Davis family, she began watching over their four-year-old son Jeffery.

"Christine did have a playful side," Orange said. "She entered the Davis home and immediately to a shine to the young Jeffery. She pretended like she was a monster and began tickling the young boy. Jeffery's parents had no reason to suspect that she would do harm to him. Christine was a little slow but was young and could project a sweet persona when she needed."

Hours later, however, Jeffery's mother would come home to see Christine standing over her young son with a glass of Kool-Aid.

Her son was not breathing.

"What happened?" Jeffery's mother screamed.

"He stopped breathing."

"Don't just stand there," she screamed again. "Call an ambulance!"

Jeffery would be pronounced dead on arrival at the hospital.

An autopsy was performed but the cause of death was found to be a pre-existing heart condition which caused the life-sustaining organ to expand to an extremely unhealthy size. Upon further inspection, however, the coroner determined that the heart inflammation was not enough to cause this kind of sudden death. Failing to discover any other notable injuries or oddities of the child's physiology, the case was chalked up as a mysterious death.

Three days later, however, Christine would by hired to look after a young boy named Joseph Spring. His parents would be going to the funeral of the young Jeffery.

They had no idea that Christine was responsible for Jeffery's death.

Christine followed the same modus operandi as she did with young Jeffery. She was immediately able to charm the child with her own child-like qualities. She saw that the boy was interested in trucks and started to play "demolition derby" with him. His parents were satisfied that the child would be safe in her care and went to the funeral of Jeffery, their nephew who had been killed by their babysitter.

Joseph's parents left and after a few hours, the boy fell. He began crying and screaming which set off Christine.

"She couldn't handle frustration of any kind," Orange said. "She would pace back and forth, telling the boy to 'shush' but of course he doesn't listen. She can't handle it."

Christine experienced auditory hallucinations when her frustrations reached a peak. The voices in her head would tell her to 'kill' and 'make the child quiet.' She could not differentiate between the real voices and the voices in her head.

So she grabbed the nearest blanket and began suffocating the young boy.

"She was schizophrenic," Orange said. "You combine that with her low IQ and it is the recipe for disaster if she is watching a young child. She cannot parse out her rational thoughts from the voices in her head. This would lead to tragic consequences."

Like before, the coroner was puzzled by the death of a young and healthy boy. He speculated that

the cause of death might very well have been some undocumented, possibly new kind of viral infection. This theory would also account for the death of Jeffery Davis as well as Joseph since neither of them bore any marks of violence. Once again the coroner closed the case, dismissing it as a complete mystery.

"No one suspected Christine of anything," Orange said. "Her dumb and sweet persona actually worked in her favor. Nobody could suspect any malice to come out of her. She would smile and come across like an overgrown child. She didn't fit the mold of a child killer. On the surface, she had no sinister aspect about her."

Christine's reign of terror continued to go on unchecked as she moved to the town of Perry. This go around, however, she would become a caretaker rather than a babysitter. An elderly man named Wilbur Swindle needed someone to look after him and find a willing candidate in the smiling Christine.

On her first day of employment, however, the old man would be found dead.

Once again, the coroner would drop the ball, dismissing the old man's death due to a heart attack brought on by the failing health of old age.

There was no police inquiry.

"The killing of Wilbur Swindle seemed to be an anomaly in Christine's pattern of murder," Orange said. "For whatever reason, she had targeted young children. So the killing of Swindle looked to be a murder of opportunity. He probably did or said something to upset her. He was old and feeble and could easily be smothered down by the obese Christine."

TIME AWAY

Some time passed and Christine was contacted by her step-sister Geneva Daniels. Geneva had an eight-month-old daughter. They had not seen each other in awhile and Geneva invited Christine to go on a shopping trip.

On the way home, Geneva remembered that she needed some diapers. She parked outside the local store and ran in for only a minute.

She made the mistake of leaving the crying baby with Christine.

Moments later, an ear-piercing scream could be heard from the car. The louder the child screamed, the more agitated Christine became.

"Once again, her low frustration threshold kicked in," Orange said. "She simply never learned how to handle a stressful situation. What would seem like a mundane situation to a normal person, a baby crying, would seem like a life or death scenario to Christine. The more the baby cried, the less control she felt. Then she had to lash out."

She placed the baby's fuzzy blanket over its mouth and held it there until she stopped crying.

Her step-sister returned to the car only to find her eight-month-old baby girl in a lifeless heap in the arms of Christine.

Christine herself was crying, flailing her arms and hyperventilating.

"She stopped breathing," Christine said.

Her step-sister didn't suspect Christine at all.

Neither did the police.

"That is one of the reasons why Christine was able to commit these murders," Orange said. "She mastered the art of smothering, particularly with a loose material. It doesn't leave behind any marks or clues. It simply blocks the airways and the coroners are left grasping at straws."

JUSTICE AT LAST...

Christine's long, lengthy string of supernatural luck in avoiding suspicion came to a bitter and crushing end in the year of 1982.

Christine would meet a family who employed her to watch their ten-week-old son named Travis Coleman.

Travis would die under her care but initially, they held no suspicions toward Christine.

The coroner's exam would reveal that the child's death had not been some viral infection or cerebral swelling, but rather a strangulation!

Christine would go immediately to the hospital and check herself in. Her hypochondriac tendencies kicking in, she demanded that doctors find out what was wrong with her. She insisted that she was passing along a virus that was killing the children.

The physicians would find nothing wrong with her physically.

Finally, Christine told the doctor to call the police.

"I have something I want to tell them," she said.

Christine did not lie this time when faced with police questioning. She said she had killed her child using a method she described as "smotheration."

She then confessed to killing the other children using similar methods.

"Christine probably wanted to be caught at this point," Orange said. "She would confess while she was at the hospital. She wanted the burden off her back. Whatever it was inside her that was forcing her to kill those children, she wanted herself to be committed. In one moment of lucidity she probably realized what a danger she was to everyone around her."

When the police pressed the young woman as to why she had done such a heinous series of deeds she responded flatly that she had heard voices in her head.

These voices told her to use "soft, thick pillows and blankets" which were the reasons why there were no discernible and incriminating marks on her victims.

Christine spoke openly of hearing strange and seductive voices telling her to "kill the baby, kill the baby, kill the baby, kill the baby!"

These words would be repeated in her head, over and over like some kind of demonic mantra.

"I don't know why I done what I done," Christine said. "The way I done it, I seen it done on TV shows. I had my own way, though. Simple and easy. No one would hear them scream."

CONVICTION

Christine was able to avoid the death penalty but was instead sentence to a life term of imprisonment with the prospect for possible parole via joint committee decision in 2007. However, in 2006 the committee came to an early decision.

She had been behaving badly in prison, engaging in unpredictable and violent outbursts. The court then dismissed her chance for parole in its entirety.

The committee judged Christine to be a threat to the public (specifically children for obvious reasons) and declared that the safest and most forward thinking course of action is to keep her imprisoned to fulfill the rest of her term.

Christine Falling remains in dark and clanking confines of the well known Homestead Prison Complex of Miami and Dade County in the state of Florida.

Her story is perhaps a penultimate warning about the dangers of undiagnosed mental health issues and childhood abuse. If the history of such heinous crime in America tells us, it's that the combination of mental frailty and a past of physical and emotional ill-treatment is a cocktail that is not just dangerous, but deadly.

CHRISTINA RIGGS

Christina Riggs had all the drugs she needed.

She had filled her prescription for the anti-depressant Elavil at the pharmacy. She had stolen morphine and potassium chloride from the hospital. Now all she had to do was follow through.

"Kids," she bellowed out from the living room table. "Vitamins!"

The two sleepy-eyed children emerged from their bedroom. Christina gave them a small amount of Elavil, dropping the pill in their mouth and watching them drink it down with a cup of water.

A few minutes later, she carried them both back to bed.

Looking down at her two young children, she began to sob.

Shelby, just two years old, in her pink jumper. Justin, five years old, in his white pajamas with battleship designs.

I have to do this. Things will only get worse for them.

THE GREATEST TABOO

Christina Marie Riggs was twenty-six years when she decided to kill her children.

"A mother is supposed to protect her own children," Riggs' Defense Attorney John Wesley Hall Jr. said. "And here she didn't and it doesn't make sense. Two defenseless children that didn't know what was coming."

After Christina sedated her children, she proceeded with her plan of injecting them with potassium chloride. She knew that the drug was administered for lethal injection executions and would stop the heart within minutes.

What she didn't know was that the drug had to be administered in a diluted form. If it is injected without any dilution, it will burn through the skin then burst through the vein.

Ignorant of the consequences, Christina injected the lethal cocktail into her son Justin first.

She wanted a painless death. She did not want her children to go through life suffering like she did.

But then her son woke up screaming.

The potassium chloride she injected was binding and burning through his blood vessel linings.

He cried and cried and wouldn't stop.

Christina began crying herself...

CHILDHOOD TRAUMA

Christina Riggs had a troubled childhood growing up in Oklahoma City, OK.

She was separated from her brothers and sisters after her parent's divorce. Raised alone by her mother, she detailed in a prison diary sexual abuses that took place in her childhood.

She wrote how her stepbrother sexually abusing her from the age of seven to thirteen. At the age of thirteen, she was molested by a neighbor as well.

By the time she entered her teenage years, Christina was obese, using food as an emotional outlet. She also began abusing alcohol and marijuana.

"She indulged in overeating because she didn't want to appear attractive," forensic psychologist Paula Orange said. "That behavior was part of a psychological response to being molested. 'If I become fat and ugly then he won't want me anymore.' No one will bother me, no one will hurt me."

In her teenage years, however, Christina began to use sex as a way to get what she wanted, which was love.

"It isn't uncommon for abused young women to become very promiscuous," Orange said. "It is learned behavior. She became defective, if you will, and should have gotten help. Unfortunately, this is not a good recipe for someone who wants to have a healthy stable relationship and raise children."

"I felt that no boy liked me because of my weight," Christina wrote in her journal. "So I became sexually promiscuous because I thought that was the only way I could have a boyfriend."

She became pregnant by the age of sixteen but gave the baby boy up for adoption.

After high school, Christina went to a vocational school to become a licensed practical nurse (LPN). She obtained employment as a home care nurse and then later worked full-time at a VA hospital.

Her dating life remained steady albeit unsuccessful. She went from one man to the next, dating a Navy ensign named Jon Riggs and a bouncer before meeting Timothy Thompson. Thompson was an Air Force private at Tinker Air Force Base.

Three years after her first child, Christina would become pregnant with Timothy's baby. She informed Timothy her pregnancy the day before he was to be discharged from the Air Force.

Timothy, however, did not take the news well. He would not accept responsibility and moved back to his native Minnesota.

"Chrissy's luck with men was about zero to nothing," Carol Thomas, Christina's mother said.

But while her relationship ended with Timothy, Christina hooked back up with Jon Riggs who returned home after being on leave with the Navy.

"It was great," Christina wrote. "He felt the baby's first kick. As far as he was concerned, it was his baby."

Justin Thomas was born on June 7th, 1992.

"As I held Justin in my arms and looked into his little face, I became so scared," Christina wrote. "Would I be a good Mom? Could I give him all he needed?"

Riggs would move in with Christina and the two hoped for the best. Christina would become pregnant again and the couple would marry in July of 1993.

But misfortune would strike again as Christina would suffer a miscarriage on her wedding night.

The marriage would go south from there as Christina alternated between being depressed to having suicidal thoughts. She blamed her mental state on her birth control medication and a doctor gave her the anti-depressant Prozac.

The medication worked for a while but then Christina inexplicably stopped taking the drug. She kept her sadness to herself and didn't want to burden others with her problems.

"She's always been that way," Christina's mother said. "If I pushed her hard she might get mad and tell me what was going on."

By 1994, Christina would become pregnant and deliver a healthy baby girl in December named Shelby. This would mark the high point of Christina's life as "Sissie" and "Bubbie", the two nicknames for her children, brought immeasurable joy into her life.

She would write that it was the happiest time of her life as both she and Jon cried when they held their new baby in their arms. Things were happy for once in her life.

Christina continued to work as a vocational nurse and was assigned to work at a triage station which served to help the victims of the Oklahoma City Federal Building terrorist bombing. She would suffer post-traumatic stress disorder as a result. Later at her trial, the prosecuting attorneys would argue that the hospital had no record of Christina serving after the bombing. This may be nitpicking as authorities were lenient with record keeping during that urgent situation.

STRESS AND STRAIN

A year later, the couple would move to Sherwood, Arkansas to be closer to Christina's mother, Carole.

Carole worked as a food service worker at Baptist Hospital and Christina was able to find a job there as well, once again working as a licensed practical nurse.

The children go on to have ailments that would stress out the already fragile Christina. Shelby would have chronic ear infections that made doctor visits a routine thing. Justin was diagnosed with attention deficit disorder and his hyper nature would grate on the nerves of his parents.

Financial difficulties and the stress of running a family would put a strain on the marriage and the couple would eventually divorce. Her husband, Jon Riggs, had a volatile temper that he eventually took out on the young Justin. Jon would punch Justin in the abdomen with such force that the young boy had to go to the emergency room.

Jon would then abandon the family.

"Justin would say, 'My Daddy hurt me, and then he went away,' " Christina's mother recalled.

Christina would receive limited child support from Jon and had to work long hours to provide for her family. The more hours she worked, the more she had to pay for daycare which proved to be a daily traumatic event.

Shelby would cry as Christina would leave her at the facility.

"She was beating on the glass, yelling, 'Mama! Mama!' " Christina recalled.

Despite her increased efforts, Christina could not get ahead financially. She began writing bad checks. Bills remained unpaid. Car insurance. Car registration. Lights and utilities.

"I started out in a boat with a small hole," Christina said. "But the hole kept getting bigger, and no matter how hard you bail, you keep sinking. I was tired and I gave up. Suicide seemed like the only thing."

A HISTORY OF MENTAL ILLNESS

Christina had a cousin that killed herself. Her mother had also tried to kill herself when Christina was a baby. Her grandmother was committed to a mental institution.

But Christina would outdo them all in one fateful night.

"Just speaking in general," Orange said. "When mothers kill their children they do not poison them. In the case of Christina, she was applying what she thought would be a lethal injection."

But even with a history of mental illness in the family, nobody could have predicted how the sweet and caring Christina could commit such a heinous crime.

"Chrissy always wanted to help people," Christina's sister, Elizabeth Nottingham said. "She was always helping someone."

But Nottingham had some valuable psychological insight on her sister. She was a mental health counselor and had been close to Christina.

She wanted to know what drove her sister to kill her own children. After her sister's arrest, she began fishing around her house, looking for some kind of clue, a sign that everyone had missed.

"I was almost hoping to find that she wasn't a good parent," Nottingham said. "Then I could be mad at her. You know, I went through her house with a fine toothed comb. All the chemicals were locked away. The food was in the refrigerator. Even pictures of their fathers was in their room above each of their beds. She was great with the kids."

MORE TROUBLE WITH MEN

What Christina's sister would find out was that she simply could not find a decent man. That one relationship where everything would be ideal.

After her divorce from Jon, Christina would enter into another relationship which again would not go well.

"The guy didn't just break her heart," Nottingham said. "But took her credit card. I mean, it's one thing to have someone dump you, it's another to have someone rip you off and leave you destitute too."

After this break-up, Christina would sit at her dining room table both broke and broken-hearted. She had no man in her life. She had no means to pay her family's bills.

Seeing only dark lights ahead, Christina would lapse into a deep depression. She went to her doctor again who prescribed her more Prozac which used irregularly.

"She may have stopped taking the Prozac when she killed the babies," Orange said. "When someone just stops that medication cold-turkey it can have some side effects like increased irritability, irrational mood changes, and an even deeper depression."

"So she had the perfect storm brewing," Nottingham said. "She had depression, she had all of these personal failures. You know, people talk about having rainy days and Mondays. And in fact 'Rainy days and Mondays' was the CD that was in her CD player."

BACK TO THAT FATEFUL NIGHT

Christina had to kill herself. Her emotional bank account had been overdrawn for years.

But she couldn't stand the thought of leaving her children alone.

"If she left the kids behind," Hall Jnr said. "She was afraid that the children would be separated, go to their father's, for instance, and be split up."

"She just thought there was no other way out," Nottingham said. "She thought that no one else would take care of her kids. And that they would be better off, in her mind, she was saving them from future sadness."

With Justin screaming in pain, Christina panicked. She began sobbing but whatever remain of her maternal instinct kicked in and she tried to inject him with morphine.

Toxicology reports didn't reveal whether or not she did this.

But what she did do was suffocate her young son with a pillow. Sobbing, she then did the same deed to her baby daughter, Shelby.

Shaking with adrenaline and grief, Christina wobbled on shaky legs back to her living room. She took out her bottle of Elavil, an anti-depressant, and swallowed the remaining twenty-eight pills. Her nerves calming, she tried injecting the potassium chloride into her own arm.

The chemical burn right through her vein, collapsing it.

The drugs began taking effect and Christina fainted to the floor, hoping her nightmare would finally end.

THE DAY AFTER

The lethal mixture had burned a half-inch hole into Christina's arm. She didn't show up for work the next day and her mother called her cell phone and land line repeatedly.

Worried that she received no response, Carole drove to Christina's apartment and let herself in.

To her horror, she thought everyone was dead, including Christina.

"All I could do was turn around and around and scream and holler, 'No. No. No.' There's no way to describe how I felt."

Frantic, she called 911 and yelling into the phone, "My daughter and babies are dead."

Paramedics would arrive.

The children were dead.

But the medics were able to resuscitate Christina. She was transported to the intensive care unit and was kept under guard by the police.

"I had to do it so I wouldn't leave them behind," Christina was overheard saying in her hospital room. The treating physician, Dr. Jim Rice, would later testify that Christina as "combative at times" and "just incoherent and not really making any sense."

As soon as Christina became reasonably coherent, she was taken to the police station for booking.

THE INTERROGATION

On November 6th, 1997, Christina was interrogated by a Detective Jones and Detective Sharon Williams.

"Christina, what we are doing is investigating the death of your two babies. Do you want to tell us what happened?" Jones asked.

"I killed them," Christina said, crying.

"What did you say?"

"I said-"

"Did you say you killed them?"

"I'm sorry."

"How did you go about doing that?" Jones asked.

"I got some bottles and stuff from here...I need a cigarette...Darvocet."

"Are you saying that you got some medicine from the hospital?"

Christina nodded.

"Christina, how did you do it? Did you give them an injection? Did you give them a shot?"

"I tried to ... and ... I did it with Justin because I figured with him being the oldest one that he would give me more problems. So, I tried it with him and I thought it would just stop his heart. But it hurt. Oh, he said it hurt ...It didn't work, he just kept calling, 'Momma! Momma! Momma!' I just figured it was too late now because I had no place to turn back to. I cleaned out my checking account and gave my mother all the money I had."

"Christina, why did you do this?" Jones asked.

"Because I wanted to die," Christina said, crying again. "But I didn't want to die and leave my kids behind or for them to be a burden to somebody else. I didn't want them to think I didn't love them and I didn't want them to grow up separately because they have two different Daddies. And I knew if I passed away they would be fighting my Mother for custody and I didn't want that for nobody."

"You felt like you were doing it for the kids' sake?"

"In a way, yeah... my piece of mind."

"Christina, did you really want to die?"

Christina didn't respond. She continued crying.

"And you felt it would be better if your children just die with you and ... were the children already dead before you took your medicine?"

"Yes."

"How long had they been dead before you took your medicine?"

"About twenty minutes."

"About twenty minutes?"

"That's because I drank and got up and smoked a cigarette and got back and sit for a minute and...I was like, 'Okay, I'm going to do it now. I can't turn back now because you've already killed Justin.' And ... so I did it."

"What time did you give them the medicine? Do you remember?"

"Justin about 10:15 or 10:30."

"10:15 or 10:30 in the morning?"

"No, in the evening."

"Oh, in the evening?"

"Last night."

"Okay."

"Then I smoked another cigarette and waited," Christina paused. "And suffocated Shelby."

"You suffocated Shelby? What did ... how did you suffocate her?"

"I put a pillow over her head."

"Okay, Did you ... Had you given her any medicine at all, or ... any of the Morphine or the Potassium Chloride?"

"I slipped them ... I made them drink half of an Elavil because I figured that would make them sleep a little bit better so that it wouldn't wake them."

"So, Shelby, you killed her with a pillow. You suffocated her. And what about the little boy. How did you do him?"

"I gave him the medicine and when it didn't work."

"You suffocated him too?"

"Yes."

"With a pillow? Were they fighting while you suffocated them?"

"Justin did. Shelby a little bit but not much," Christina began to cry again.

"When did you decide to do this, Christina? On what day did you decide to do this?"

"Uh ... the best I remember it was Sunday night or Saturday night because we was out talking and this and that and the other ... and they caught me."

"Who caught you?"

"I was depressed. I was thinking about what was going on in my life and that things aren't always working for me and..."

"When did you get those drugs from the hospital?"

"When? Yesterday."

"Yesterday? You mean the day that you killed them? Is that the day that you got the drugs? The last was it ... "

"Was it the last day that you worked at the hospital or the day before that? "I think ..."

"When you got ... "

"I got the drugs and I gave them to my kids. That's the only drugs that I had in my hand. And I know that there was three Valiums in a vial in there, but there wasn't enough to even cover the jar up and put it in my pocket and bring them home. And I know I should have thought better ... had somebody rinsing with me, but ... they were just what came home in my pockets."

"Did you know what you were going to do when you took the drugs from the hospital? Did you have intentions of giving them to your children? And how many days did you think about this before you killed your children?"

"About three weeks. Two weeks."

"Two or three weeks. In other words, you've been thinking about doing this for the last two or three weeks? What made you decide to just go ahead and do it?"

"I just can't take it no more."

"You couldn't take it anymore."

"I felt like I was out of control," Christina said.

"Did you just feel like your life was in a mess? Had you talked to anybody about this? Your Mom or anybody?"

"I've tried to talk to people about what I feel and what I think and they were just like, 'I don't have time right now. We'll do it some other time.' So, I just got to where I don't care anymore. I tried but they can't give me no help."

"So you just felt like nobody was listening to you? Okay, Christina ...Christina, do you have anything more to say about your babies or anything? "I wish I hadn't done it now."

Christina would then go on an incoherent ramble, explaining how she saw her mother riding down an escalator with a bunch of old people. The detectives, however, got the damning evidence they needed and ended the interrogation.

PRISON AND JAIL

Christina would find a hostile environment in prison. The majority of her fellow prisoners were women who were taken away from their children by force. They had contempt for Christina's crime.

One inmate spat in her face and her life was threatened.

Christina was then moved to an isolated cell where she remained until her trial.

She would be charged with two counts of first-degree murder which was punishable by death in the state of Arkansas.

"We tried to show that she was under extreme emotional disturbance," Hall Jr said. "To justify either not imposing the death penalty or hopefully finding her guilty of second-degree murder."

"I just hope that out of all her misery," Nottingham said. "The sadness of our family. That we can shed some light on the causes of this for other people and that maybe they'll be able to look at the symptoms and look at the situations and maybe intervene for someone else."

But the prosecuting attorney, as well as the community, believed that Christina was guilty of performing a selfish act, an act wherein she tried to free herself from motherhood.

The most damning evidence at the trial, aside from the interrogation tapes, would be the account of the physicians.

One doctor would testify that it would take three to six minutes to suffocate someone to death. Because of that time period, the jurors would be able to envision how Christina commit a willful act of murder. Christina had, in essence, a struggling toddler under her pillow for about three to six minutes...suffocating to death.

"They just wanted her to be evil," Nottingham said of the prosecuting attorney's intent. "It was easier that way."

"Essentially, what the jury saw was that she was self-centered," argued Pulaski Prosecuting Attorney Larry Jegley. "That she viewed the children as an inconvenience and an interference with what she wanted to pursue. She placed her interests above those of the children."

Jegley argued that Christina was a self-centered and premeditated murderer. He brought up the fact that she had locked the children up in the house (according to a neighbor) in order that she could go out to a Karaoke party. He urged the jury not to buy into her manipulation to feel sorry for her. "There were lots of people who have it worse than she did."

The jury would side with the prosecution and find Christina guilty after a very short deliberation period.

THE IRONY

Christina Riggs would be sentenced to death by lethal injection via potassium chloride...The same method that she used to try to kill her children and herself.

"It was a cruel irony that they finished what she started," Hall Jr said. "Almost the exact same way except she was strapped down to a table."

Christina would appeal the sentencing but did so with reluctance. She wanted to die.

"I'll be with my children and with God," Christina said. "I'll be where there's no more pain. Maybe I'll find some peace."

Her defense attorney John Wesley Hall Jr was allowed to witness the execution.

"You can see their face," Hall Jr said. "It allows them to say their last words. The face changes color as the drugs take effect. You turn gray. The skin turns gray. And it's rather shocking to watch it happen."

"She was so depressed that it became this black sheet over her eyes that she couldn't see through," Orange said. "She wanted to spare her own children from the kind of life that she had. She had lost complete hope and really over thought things. That's how her depression warped her. It warped her enough to think that she was doing her children a favor by killing them."

Christina was sent to death row and was haunted by the memories of her children. She openly stated that she tried "not to think about them" because when she did it was like someone "ripping them away from her all over again."

"A lot of regret," Christina said. "That's what goes through my mind, day-in, day-out. God's punishing me. He let me live so I would suffer."

Riggs was flown in from McPherson Jail to Cummins in order to prep for her execution. She would be administered the lethal injection at 9:28 PM CDT on May 2nd, 2000.

"No words can express just how sorry I am for taking the lives of my babies," Riggs said in a prepared statement. "No way I can make up for or take away the pain I have caused everyone who knew and loved them. I love you, my babies."

SUSAN SMITH : CHILD KILLER

CARLA THOMPSON

Looking Back: Susan Smith, Abuse Survivor and Child Killer

Filicide. Infanticide. Prolicide. Neonaticide. We have many words to talk about the murder of children. One of the top five ways a child under the age of 5 can die is by homicide, and 61% of those deaths were the fault of the children's parents. In any given year in the United States, the FBI estimates that, on average, there are 450 filicide cases on average. Someone who is guilty of filicide is someone who has been found to have murdered their own child or children. Before the age of 8, the majority of filicide cases are committed by the mother, and after the age of 8, death by the father becomes the majority. Michael and Alex Smith, the sons of Susan Smith, were both under 8 years of age, and unfortunately they both fall under the typical infanticide statistics.

The idea of a mother who kills her children will always capture the attention of the nation, and in some cases the entire world will tune in as they did in Smith's situation, at first with sympathy and then with outrage. Why would someone commit the most unspeakable of acts? How could a mother kill her child? In 1994, these questions were asked of Susan Smith, a young woman living in Union of South Carolina during an unusual case. In the slightly more than 22 years following the event, we can't be entirely certain what she was thinking that day. She has said herself that she wasn't in her right mind when she murdered her sons, and since then she has blamed her actions on past traumas. Rumors flew, of course, that Smith had wanted to be with the son of the wealthy owner of the Conso Products company where Smith worked. His name was Tom Findley, and he didn't want children of his own nor to be a stepfather and that this facts was her true motivation to drown her children. There is evidence that a breakup letter from Findley existed to support this theory. Smith vehemently denies that this was the case, but with so few real answers and, as Smith is a proven liar, it is hard to determine fact from fiction. At the time, Smith and the boys' father, David Smith, had been separated and co-parenting. One can only sympathize with the father, who likely blames himself, even today.

Other writers have claimed that she is battling her demons while in prison, and for her part Susan Smith at least pretends to be remorseful and has stated that "I was a good mother and I loved my boys." However, those who work with Smith within the prison system such as South Carolina Prisons Director Jon Ozmint paint a different picture of Smith, and say her words could not be further from the truth. They refer to her as narcissistic and say that the worldwide media attention has fed the part of her that craves fanfare. Due to reports of multiple prison violations and because she released a letter to explain herself to the public in 2015 roughly 22 years later, it seems Smith is still very ill and in dire need of further media attention. There are questions that still remain: cold blooded killer or mentally ill victim, mother desperate for help or sociopathic monster?

The Day Two Boys Died

On the day of the murders, Susan Smith, a 23-year-old mother, had been driving her sons, 3-year-old Michael and 14-month-old Alex, somewhere. Although her destination and why she packed her boys into her burgundy 1990 Mazda Protégé to begin with remain unclear, we know where the family trip ended that day. Had the bottom of a lake been Smith's plan all along, or was it like she said: had she been completely unaware of what she was doing until after she had already done it? What did she say to Michael's trusting young face as she securely fastened him into his seat, rolled up the windows, locked the doors, and put the car into neutral? What did the young boy think about while the car was filling with water and his little bother was assuredly screaming? One has to wonder if Smith thinks about this as well. After she watched her children drown in the lake she had pushed them into, fastened into her car, she located the nearest phone to call police. Did she walk to a house or store nearby? Were there witnesses, or people living in the vicinity of the boat ramp?

Smith admits that she was planning suicide before it was discovered that her boys were dead and not missing, but she never got the chance to kill herself. However, her plans were foiled. Between that conversation with police and the one nine days later when she confessed to the children's' murders, it is unclear what was preventing her from ending her life. There is speculation originating from her lawyers that Smith was planning to die alongside her children, but ditched when the thought of drowning became too overwhelming.

Although her story continued to change minutely, during the initial investigation, Smith blamed an armed black man and alleged that he had stolen her car with her kids in the backseat. She gave a detailed description of what had happened: the black man had forced her out of the car at a deserted intersection where she had stopped for a red light. These details eventually became the undoing of her case. With tears running down her face, Smith begged for her children to be returned safely, all the while knowing exactly where they were. Something about her body language unsettled detectives, who were doing all they could to locate her children. By alleging that a black man had done this to her, she raised already high racial tensions in the local area and across the country, selfishly damaging more lives to try and protect her own. When her lie was found out, black communities were justifiable livid.

When investigators checked the intersection, and noticed that the light turns red only when another car is waiting on the crossroads, they realized there was something suspicious about her story. Former chief of the South Carolina Law Enforcement Division, Robert Stewart, had this to say about their findings: "We were able to show, at one point, that her story could not have happened at that intersection because she said nobody was there ... In order for the light to be red, a car would have had to activate the pressure pad on the intersecting street to make her light red." Emboldened by this finding, Stewart told Smith that the security camera at that intersection doesn't show the footage that should have been there if her story was true. This bit of lying, and an accompanying threat to take the information to the press, brought out Smith's confession.

Tommy Pope and Keith Giese were the two prosecutors assigned to Susan Smith's case, and they began to prepare for the most famous case of their careers. After reviewing the evidence, they agreed with Stuart's supposition that Smith's story had large inconsistencies or could have been entirely fabricated. Pope discusses the letter that Smith's lover, Tom Findley had written and Smith's motives, by saying: "He writes her a Dear Jane letter saying 'you're a nice girl, but I really don't want kids,' ... rather than tell her the truth, he kind of tied it to the kids. I think that what happened in her mind is she thought with the kids gone, then there is a chance for me with the boss's son." It was Pope and Giese who initially pushed for the death sentence for the conclusion of Smith's case.

Her Trial, and Her Time in Prison

Although it is necessary to mention that most people suffering from mental illnesses do not commit a single crime in their lifetimes, anyone who kills a child or commits filicide is most likely mentally ill in some respect. Her highly skilled lawyers for the case, David Bruck and Judy Clarke, put forth the defense that she was mentally unstable, and pointed to multiple mental health conditions such as severe depression and dependent personality disorder. Although the prosecution is on record for saying that they didn't believe that argument, the defense did have a good point: Smith had for years suffered various sexual abuses at the hands of her stepfather, and could have been driven to the point of insanity.

Despite any mitigating factors that Smith might have had, drowning is one of the worst ways to die as it takes several minutes of pure terror before the body begins to painfully shut down. The prosecutors showed the court a video of a sinking car recreation, and the court watched in horror as it took a silent six minutes before the car completely submerged. Giese, one of the prosecutors said: "Looking back on it now after 20 years, it was one of the most gut-wrenching, moving experiences I have ever felt in a courtroom ... Tommy and I had done plenty of other murder cases together, so it wasn't like we hadn't seen tragedy in a courtroom. But I was fighting back tears." The image of two young children dying that way at the hands of their mother is haunting. The disturbing way in which she killed her children and the actions she took to hide her crime was proof enough to the judge that she was aware enough of her transgressions that she deserved to be punished for them. Although Pope and Giese pushed for the death sentence, the court sentenced her to life in prison with two counts of murder, with a chance for parole after 30 years, starting November 4, 2024. Since the conclusion of the trial there have been times when prosecutors have called for a death sentence, despite the fact that she is already in prison.

Since the conclusion of the trial, Smith wrote a letter in 2015 and held interviews in attempt to spread her version of the truth. In the letter, she writes that she isn't "the monster society thinks I am. I am far from it ... It has been hard to listen to lie after lie and not be able to defend myself. It is frustrating to say the least ... The thing that hurts me most is that people think that I hurt my children in order to be with a man. That is so far from the truth. There was no motive as it was not even a planned event." She goes on to say that she pretended not to know of the boys' fates because she didn't want to cause their loved ones undue distress. Somehow, she assumed that the idea of being kidnapped by a man was less traumatizing. This letter shows that she is still incapable of empathy, and wrongfully understands what other people might be thinking or feeling, or what they might need.

In prison, Susan Smith has had a tumultuous time. She has been racking up prison violations, including two counts of sexual misconduct with two prison guards, Houston Cagle and Alford J. Rowe, although this number is suspected of being higher. Both known men were released from their positions and barred from working within the criminal justice system in South Carolina ever again. Smith has developed several other relationships, including one with a bank robber who has a life sentence and a long distance partnership with a man who also serves as her benefactor. Over the years this nameless benefactor has sent thousands of dollars and shelled out for some expensive hospital stays for her. She has also harmed herself on various occasions by flaying her own skin. A woman who met Smith in the Leath Correctional Institution has said that some of the approximately fifteen self-harm scars are "some three inches long" and that Smith has said "You don't feel pain when you cut. Cutting takes all the pain away". Throughout 2010 and 2015, she was caught with illegal substances, including prescription pills. And again in 2012, she collected more infractions for "unauthorized use of an inmate's pin credit." According to Ozmint, prison has done nothing to change her character for the better unlike other murderers that he has worked with in his time as South Carolina Prisons Director.

She has appealed her sentencing before, but as her own representative Smith has done herself no favors. Her appeal was based on her perceived violation of her "Amanda Rights", by which she meant, of course, her "Miranda Rights". She claims that was forced into a confession without her attorney being present. However, with such ignorance of the legal system, it is easy to see why her appeal was rejected. On top of her legal illiteracy, the evidence still weighs heavily against her. During her attempt to have her sentencing overturned, she purported that she was a victim of "battered woman's syndrome", but her ex-husband and the boys' father was cleared of any criminal offenses. Smith has spent a long time in prison already, but has shown little to no signs that she is any stage of rehabilitation and despite multiple accrued infractions, her initial candidacy for parole is set for November 4th, 2024. Smith will be 53.

Susan Smith: The Girl and Woman Before the Filicide
Although her past traumas should not be used as an excuse for her crimes, it is worth noting that Susan Smith has

never had an easy life. She was born on the 26th of September in 1971, and her full name had been Susan Leigh Vaughan. Her father took his own life when she was just six years old, and you could surmise that her life with her single mother was unstable. She attempted suicide at least twice, once when she was thirteen and again after she graduated from high school. Beverly Russell, Smith's stepfather somewhat nonchalantly admitted on the stand that he sexually abused her when she was a teenager. He also stated that he had had sex with her when she was an adult, and the consensual part of his claim is dubious. This is a man who stated on the stand that he would never have raped his stepdaughter had he known she was at risk of becoming a murderer: "Had I known what the result of my sin would be, I would have mustered the strength to behave according to my responsibility," Russell acknowledged. One has to wonder if Russell faced any charges for his confessed sexual abuse of a minor, but there seems to be no evidence suggesting that he faced penalties for his serious transgressions. Clearly Susan Smith was surrounded by poisonous familial relationships.

Sometime shortly after high school, Smith married her now ex-husband David Smith, with whom she had Michael and Alex. She would have been approximately nineteen or twenty years old when she was pregnant with her first child. The relationship was described in much the same way as Smith's personal relationships up until then had been: poisonous and rocky. They seemed to fight regularly and had a history of separation due to mutual accusations of cheating. She was certainly a troubled person, and Smith has since used her abusive upbringing and unstable personal life as an excuse for the horrendous crime she committed. Many people live absolutely terrible lives and do not go on to murder their children, however, and so the judicial system has continued to believe she belongs in prison for the full extent of her sentencing.

A Damaged Community

During the week and a half that this community thought two small boys had been kidnapped, they had to put up with the wide scale media that descended upon them, including news vans and helicopters. The media used the helicopters to project signals to spread the story back to their outlet's headquarters, and the sound of the choppers kept small children awake late into the night. The town of Union was small with approximately 10,000 people living there. News spread quickly, and rumors happened easily. They had to watch their town be discussed on national and international televisions. It was an entirely stressful process that many residents wished to not live through again. Likely the stresses of the case were enough that chief Robert Stewart felt justified in the deceptions he created in order to trick Smith into confessing, and there were no reprimands of his actions. He has been quoted as saying: "There was never any another[sic] suspect ... Susan Smith was a conniving, manipulative person," in defense of his actions. When the Union County Sheriff at the time, a man named Howard Wells, announced their findings of Smith's guilt, Stewart recalls that there was an audible gasp from the crowd. It was as if the nightmare was happening for a second time:

once when the community learned two boys may have been kidnapped, and again when they learned that the mother begging them for help had been the children's killer.

The searchers, who were community members as well as divers from the Department of Natural Resources, expanded their area of search, which included going further into the lake. It was initially thought that the car, should it be down there, would have traveled approximately 60ft into the lake before stopping. When the car was eventually found, it was a full 120ft from shore and was beneath 18ft of water. The grisly discoveries rocked what had once been a quiet community. Fred Delk, who was in charge of a downtown revitalization committee and had once had a career in media, was appointed to train local citizens in the ways to speak to the media. Maintaining the image of Union as a peaceful, friendly town was important, and they worried that they would be misrepresented if they didn't act quickly. Whenever there were televised conferences, they were shot only in front of newer houses with green, well-trimmed lawns in order to present the community as a perfect southern town. What followed was the news media's complete disregard of the local bylaws and parking spots. Parking tickets were ignored because the media outlets could pay for them, and so they weren't a deterrent to illegal parking. Delk resorted to using borrowed boots in order to prevent the news vans from following people around. Susan Smith's mother was commonly harassed or bothered.

People from across the country come to the spot where Smith murdered her children to lay flowers or to take pictures of the scene. On the same boat ramp where Susan Smith's boys lost their lives, other people have died of similar circumstances. One entire family died accidentally while stopping to look at the memorials that the town had placed there in honor of Smith's two children. The ramp was torn down only a few years after Smith's trial as a lasting, physical legacy of what she had done to her children and their community. The loss of the ramp was not the only consequence of Smith's actions, however. The world was enraged and confused by her actions, and the local community was impacted worse of all. The downtown center of the town is a stretch of four blocks, and in the center near town hall was where Smith told the nation that a black man had stolen her car and children. Store owners in the area felt overrun at times, and since the incident there are visitors who still drive the route Susan Smith would have taken to the lake.

The mayor of Union, a man named Harold Thompson, is the town's first African-American mayor, and in his mind the trial and deaths weigh heavily on the town's history. While those who visit the area today will find a green, quiet southern town like any other, the incidents that happened back in 1994 remain in the thoughts of all residents. Thompson notes that in all the time since Smith's confession, there was never a formal apology given to the black community of Union. The mayor recalls that black residents were questioned at random by the police about the Smith's missing boys, and he says that "situations like that create problems between the black community and law enforcement ... [black residents] were hurt, but their hurt wasn't channeled towards the white community. It was more channeled toward the police department." It could cause future issues between the community and law enforcement, because if the trust isn't there and someone needs help, they are less likely to call police.

Despite all reasons not to, it seems that Union has started to shake its appalling history. When asked about the murder this many years on, someone people have to be reminded that it ever happened. Fortunately, Union will be able to return to a more peaceful reputation. However, there are still times when outsiders to the community ask residents questions or treat them differently because of the dark fame Susan Smith had won. The echoes of what she did will continue to rebound for a little more it seems, before they fade completely.

The Legacy of Filicide

Susan Smith will forever haunt the minds of her community. Why did a mother who at least seemed to be successfully co-parenting her two young children suddenly deposit them into the bottom of a neighborhood lake? Having a history of abuse, be it physical or sexual, does not mean that you will go on to commit a crime of any kind, but for some individuals it does lend a hand in getting them into trouble. Statistics on filicide cases in the United States point to the fact that psychological and physical abuse of children often occur before their deaths at the hands of their parents. It would be speculation at this point to guess at whether or not Michael and Alex had been in a similar situation, but how much stock can be put into Susan Smith's claim that she was a "good mother" and "loved [her] boys"?

Does Smith deserve to be eligible for parole on November 4th, 2024? As Jon Ozmint, the former director of the South Carolina Department of Corrections, has said: even the coldest criminals who have committed the most heinous crimes eventually come around and try to be better people, but we haven't seen that from Smith. She continues to cause trouble in prison, and while her self-harm may point to some layer of guilt, her actions towards others and herself continue to be hurtful. Ozmint notes that "part of the problem is the media writing stories about her. She is truly a narcissist, and she thrives on the media's attention. Someone like that, I didn't want to feed that narcissism. Other than passing her on the yard, I wouldn't give her any extra, undue attention." He goes on to say that she is a heavy weight on the criminal justice system. Perhaps Pope and Giese, her prosecutors, were right in seeking the death penalty for her. Alive, however, she only has more time to learn to regret what she has done to her children and to the hearts and minds of the Union community and to the nation.

Filicide or the murder of one's own child by one's own hands is inarguably despicable. It is often the crime of a mentally disturbed mother for an additional reason, which can sometimes remain unknown. It is important to remember that Susan Smith suffered from mental illnesses, childhood abuses, and a rocky relationship with a man who was supposed to love her. She has documented narcissistic traits and known infidelity issues. And she believed she was a good and caring mother. What exactly happened in her mind on October 25th, 1994, we may never know for certain, because even Susan is unaware of what she had been thinking that day. It is fortunate that at least her two young boys, Michael and Alex, did not rest eternally in a watery grave and that their loved ones were able to learn the truth about their untimely and ghastly deaths.

BABY KILLER : THE TRUE STORY OF KATHLEEN FOLBIGG

CHELSEA HILTON

Kathleen Folbigg was a serial child killer who murdered her three infant children and was convicted for the manslaughter of a fourth. Her killings would take place over the course of an eight-year period during in which she was never suspected. She would only be discovered after her husband discovered her personal diary in which she detailed the motivations behind her killing spree.

This is her story.

A CHILDHOOD BORN IN VIOLENCE

She was born Kathleen Megan Donovan on June 14th, 1967. When she was only a year-and-half old, her father Thomas John Britton would kill her mother Kathleen by stabbing her twenty-four times two weeks before Christmas in 1968. The motive? Britton felt that his wife was neglecting the young Kathleen.

Britton was a bad news character. He had a previous conviction for slashing the throat of his first wife before Kathleen's mother. He also had numerous children out of wedlock and had a history of violent crimes.

The murder was witnessed by a neighbor. She stated that Kathleen's father confronted her mother Mary on the steps onside their home. He would brutally stab her to death then bend down to whisper his apologies to his dying bride.

"I'm sorry, darling. I had to do it."

Thomas then stood back up and looked at his neighbor, dropping the bloody weapon to the ground.

"I had to kill her," he said. "Because she'd kill my child."

Her father would be arrested the day after the murder and the young Kathleen was placed into the care of an aunt and uncle. It was here that she was rumored to have suffered sexual abuse.

On July 18th, 1970, Kathleen was removed from her aunt and uncle's home and placed into the Bidura Children's Home. Four months later, she would be moved into another foster care home and this time it would be permanent. Her foster mother would describe her as a well-behaved child who got lots of attention because of her curly blonde hair. But Kathleen would mostly keep to herself and rarely expressed her feelings or emotions.

"Folbigg would suffer from what is called an attachment disorder," forensic psychiatrist Paula Orange said. "People who have suffered in her circumstances usually turn to alcohol or substance abuse to medicate themselves. In Kathleen's case, she would eventually turn toward violence toward her own children."

Kathleen would remain in the foster home until she left school at age fifteen, working a series of menial jobs. When she turned eighteen, she would be told the truth about her parents and later meet her half-sisters.

In 1987, she would marry Craig Folbigg at the age of twenty. Craig was a car salesman and she would be a stay-at-home soon to be mother. It was at this time that Kathleen began writing in her diary, chronicling her thoughts and various mood swings that she kept to herself.

THE FIRST SACRIFICE

Kathleen would give birth to their first child, Caleb on February 1st, 1989. Caleb had difficulty breathing and was diagnosed as having a mild case of laryngomalacia also known as a "lazy larynx."

Their pediatrician would the couple every assurance that the child would outgrow the ailment. But nineteen days after he was born, Kathleen would place Caleb to sleep and he would never wake up.

Caleb cried from midnight until 2 am that night. In the morning, Kathleen would find him dead. Initially, the doctors thought his death could be attributed to Cot Death.

"Finally Asleep!!" Kathleen would write in her diary on the day Caleb died.

Craig was oblivious to any warning signs Kathleen displayed before the death but her foster sister, Lea Bown, felt otherwise.

She stated that Kathleen hated the attention taken away from her and on the newborn child. She had a temper and hated the interruptions in her sleep. She also hated the fact that she had gained weight.

"Kathleen was a two-faced person," Orange said. "She had a reserved exterior that masked resentment she had toward certain people who made her angry. When the baby made her angry, she viewed it in the same way as an adult mistreating her."

ANOTHER BABY

Kathleen wanted another child and they continued trying to conceive. On June 3rd, 1990,their second child Patrick was born.

"This was the day that Patrick was born," Kathleen wrote in her diary. " I had mixed feelings this day. wether or not I was going to cope as a mother or wether I was going to get stressed out like <u>I did last time</u>. I often regret Caleb & Patrick, only because your life changes so much, and maybe I'm not a Person that likes change. But we will see?"

On this occasion, Craig would remain at home to take care of Kathleen and the baby for over three months. But only three days after returning to work, he would be awakened by the sound of Kathleen screaming.

He arose and found Kathleen standing above the baby's crib. His heart pounding, he saw that the baby wasn't breathing and tried to revive him with CPR.

"He rushed into Patrick's room and saw his wife standing over Patrick who was lying in his cot," the police report said. "Mr. Folbigg picked up the baby and noted faint, labored breathing. He commenced resuscitation until the ambulance arrived. Patrick regained consciousness, but was (later) found to now have epilepsy and be blind."

Kathleen could not deal with Patrick's blindness. She would leave the baby with Craig's sister, Carol Newitt and sometimes with one of her neighbors.

She would write in her diary that "Patrick and Craig would be better off if she left them."

Kathleen put on the charade, fighting off the demons in her head until one day she snapped.

That day would occur in February of 1991, when Kathleen would call Craig at his workplace, saying "It's happened again!"

Craig would arrive at the home at the same time as the paramedics. His sister was already there and when Craig entered the home he saw Patrick lying on his bed on the cot. He picked Patrick up and performed CPR, seeing that his son's lips were blue. The child was then transported to the hospital where he would be pronounced dead.

The physician on duty stated that the baby had suffered cardiac arrest but could not assign a cause to it.

Kathleen would be saddened by the death but emerge from the depression quicker than the last time. She then began to pester Craig about having another baby. Her husband agreed but only if they got SIDS specialists involved in the baby's care.

He didn't want to go through it all over again.

"The mental phenomena of Kathleen repeating the same action over and over again is born from her childhood," Orange said. "She had a very low stress threshold and would lose it whenever the baby would, in her own words, 'push her buttons.' She would smother the baby then immediately feel bad afterwards. I think she was sincere in her efforts to try and revive the children after she smothered them to death. She would immediately feel remorse but could never control the voices in her head that told her to kill."

NEW SURROUNDINGS

The couple would then move to Thornton when their new child Sarah was born on October 14th, 1992. They both held out hope that the third time would be a charm. Two children dying of SIDS was a tragedy. A third would be statistically impossible.

Or could it?

Sarah would sleep in a crib in their bedroom. She had mild sleep apnea and SIDS specialists were called in. They gave the baby use of a sleep apnea monitoring blanket. But Kathleen discontinued use of the blanket after it gave her some false alarms.

"Again, it was frustration sinking in again for Kathleen," Orange said. "The beeper would go off on the blanket and she would go nuts. Craig wouldn't know how to react to her anger. She would growl and snarl."

Kathleen was particularly nasty with Sarah who was sick more than the other babies. Craig decided to take over the care taking duties after Kathleen grew increasingly frustrated over time. He decided he would let Sarah sleep with them in their bed until she reached the age of a toddler, if need be.

But Sarah wouldn't make it to that age.

On the night of August 29th, 1993, Craig would be awakened briefly at about 1 o'clock in the morning. He saw that neither Kathleen nor the baby was in the bedroom. He went back to the sleep then heard screaming.

He woke up again to see Kathleen standing over the dead Sarah, their child lifeless.

In yet another deja vu moment, he would perform CPR to no avail as the medics arrived.

The coroner noted small cuts near Sarah's mouth and that her lungs showed damage consistent with death by asphyxiation. Nonetheless, the death was chalked up to "unknown causes."

It is now believed that Kathleen had taken Sarah out of the bedroom, smothered her to death then placed the dead baby back in the bed and faked as if she had discovered her that way.

"Sarah left us 1am," Kathleen wrote in her diary.

But Sarah would not be found dead until well after that time.

Craig would again be awoken by Kathleen's screams. The scene was repeating itself. Kathleen stood over the child's crib. Sarah laid on the cot. Dead.

Coroners would attribute her death to Sudden Infant Death Syndrome (SIDS). They would find bruises on Sarah's neck but didn't think to chalk up it to strangulation. The detective in the case would later admit that he was hamstrung by his own belief that a woman could not harm her children.

"With Sarah, all I wanted was her to shut up. And one day, she did."

After Sarah's death, Kathleen felt increasingly more isolated from Craig and the rest of his extended family.

"Why is family so important to me?" Kathleen wrote in her diary on November 13th, 1996. "I now have the start of my very own, but it doesn't seem good enough. I know Craig doesn't understand. He has the knowledge and stability and love from siblings and parents, even if he chooses to ignore them. Me I have no one but him. It seems to affect me so. Why should it matter? It shouldn't."

The isolation of being home alone and not having any children began to wear on Kathleen. She wrote of being home alone when a storm struck and feeling despondent. She wanted Craig to come home but simultaneously didn't want him there because he continued to make her feel bad about her weight.

"I actually relish in the fact he has a weight problem now. All the years of him tormenting me have come back to get him."

Kathleen would become severely depressed after Sarah's death. Their marriage would become strained and they would separate. They would eventually reconcile in early 1996 and Kathleen would once again convince Craig that they should have another baby.

A FOURTH ATTEMPT

Kathleen was still searching for her own identity according to her diary entries. After she became pregnant for a fourth time, she began questioning her own existence.

"Thirty years," Kathleen wrote. "The first five I don't really remember, the rest, I choose not to remember. The last 10-11 have been filled with trauma, tragedy, happiness and mixed emotions of all designs. If it wasn't for my baby coming soon, I'd sit and wonder again what I was put on this earth for. What contribution have I made to anyone's life?"

Both authorities and Craig were none the wiser with the doings of Kathleen. Each death was marked as natural causes and Kathleen received the obligatory sympathy from everyone around her.

Her writings in her diary, however, would paint a different picture.

"Obviously, I'm my father's daughter," Kathleen wrote she was pregnant with her fourth child. "But I think losing my temper and being frustrated and everything has passed. I now just let things happen and go with the flow. An attitude I should of had with all my children, if given the chance, I'll have it with the next one."

"Another year gone & what a year to come. I have a baby on the way, ... This time. I am going to call for help this time & not attempt to do everything myself any more – I know that that was the main Reason for all my stress before & stress made me do terrible things. Still can't sleep. Seem to be thinking of Patrick & Sarah & Caleb. Makes me generally wonder whether I am stupid or doing the right thing by having this baby. My guilt of how responsible I feel for them all, haunts me, my fear of it happening again haunts me........ What scares me most will be when Im alone with baby. How do I overcome that? Defeat that?"

Four years later after Sarah was found dead, Kathleen would give birth to her fourth child on August 7th, 1997.

Her name was Laura. Still, the idea of a fourth child was wreaking havoc on the insecure Kathleen.

"On a good note," Kathleen wrote in her diary "Craig said last night he accepts that I'm not going to be skinny again. That's wonderful, but I know deep in my heart he wants his skinny wife back. Got to start changing my life and becoming a hot-looking energetic mother for my daughter and a sexy wife for my husband."

Kathleen would seem to take to Laura moreso than she did Sarah at least from what her diary entries would indicate.

"I cherish Laura more, I miss her [Sarah] yes but am not sad that Laura is here & she isn't. Is that a bad way to think, don't know. I think I am more patient with Laura. I take the time to figure what is rong now instead of just snapping my cog. ... Wouldn't of handled another like Sarah. She's saved her life by being different."

Craig would videotape his baby giggling in the backyard pool just twenty-four hours prior to Kathleen killing her.

"Show us how you use your kickboard, darling," Craig called out to the toddler as she waded in the kiddie pool he had bought for her.

But Kathleen lurked in the background, still angry at the baby for some perceived transgression the day before.

Craig would notice how Kathleen would unleash a terrifying "growl" whenever she got frustrated with the children. This behavior would continue when Laura was born.

Her diary entries during this time would take on a darker tone. Kathleen would write about her frustrations "made her do terrible things" and of her "flashes of rage, resentment and hatred" toward her children. She complained that no control over these thoughts and felt that she needed to "ask for help.

Kathleen would also consistently make more comparisons between Laura and Sarah, often giving preference to Laura and feel guilty about it. Still, she would write of feeling irrationally angry toward Laura.

"I've done it. I lost it with her. I yelled at her so angrily that it scared her, she hasn't stopped crying. Got so bad I nearly purposely dropped her on the floor & left her. I restrained enough to put her on the floor & walk away. Went to my room & left her to cry. Was gone probably only 5 minutes but it seemed like a lifetime. I feel like the worst mother on this earth. Scared that she'll leave me know. Like Sarah did. I know I was short tempered & cruel sometimes to her & she left. With a bit of help. I don't want that to ever happen again. I actually seem to have a bond with Laura. It can't happen again. Im ashamed of myself. I can't tell Craig about it because he'll worry about leaving her with me. Only seems to happen if I'm too tired her moaning, bored, wingy sound, drives me up the wall. I truly can't wait until she's old enough to tell me what she wants."

It was all brought to a head when Laura had a cold one morning and Kathleen would give her some cough medicine.

"I feel like the worst mother on this earth," Kathleen wrote. "Scared that she [Laura] will leave me now. Like Sarah did. I knew I was short-tempered and cruel sometimes to her and she left. With a bit of help."

Kathleen would pin Laura to her high-chair and try to force-feed her some dumplings. Laura refused the food and Kathleen dropped her to the ground.

"Go to your fucking father," Kathleen sneered at the child. The crying infant would seek her father's arms but Craig would be on his way to work.

It would be the last time he would see his daughter alive.

After writing in her diary, Kathleen would smother her child to death. She then called the ambulance, once again switching from tormented killer to the frantic mother.

"My baby's not breathing," Kathleen screamed at the dispatcher. "I've had three SIDS deaths already...I've had three go already."

The medics would arrive on scene to find Kathleen "performing CPR on her daughter on the breakfast bar."

They took over resuscitation duties but saw that the child was not breathing and had no pulse.

Laura would be pronounced dead on February 27th, 1999.

Craig would describe Kathleen as going through a "broken sparrow" routine after each of the child's death. On each occasion, he would awaken to Kathleen's bone-chilling screams and then see her standing over the crib. After the baby would be declared dead, she would pack all of their belongings away, take their pictures down and never mention the child's name ever again.

Detective Sergeant Bernard Ryan was sent to investigate Laura's death but this time he did not dismiss it as another "cot death."

He put Kathleen and Craig through the routine interview but grew suspicious when he discovered that this was their fourth child to die from SIDS or something similar.

Kathleen then left Craig without warning. She moved out of the family home and took only a small amount of possessions with her.

Craig, chalked up her abandonment of the marriage to the child deaths, began to clean up the house when he made a shocking discovery as he opened up his wife's bedside drawer.

He began reading through the passages, reading one disturbing confession after the other.

Craig began to dry heave as he realized that it was his wife all along. She had killed their children.

The diary that she left behind turned out to be one of many as Kathleen had already thrown away a few.

In reading the passages it became apparent that she did want children to "prove she could do it, just like other women could," and she seemed to be an anticipation of the newborn coming into her life. "We're all waiting, little one, when will you come?"

But like her foster sister described, Kathleen felt frustrated with the daily duties of being a mother. She did not like how the baby was always the center of atttention and felt as if she was "abandoned."

"I'm in a family but never felt like part of it," Kathleen wrote. "I have wild mood swings. I watch swim in a tank to try and get peace. I don't know, how do I conquer this? Help is what I want."

She wrote that of her worries that Craig would leave her and felt bad when he teased her about her weight gain after the pregnancies. He once rejected sex from her when she was pregnant.

"He is always flirting with other women," Kathleen wrote. "Craig's roving eye will always be of concern to me. Must lose extra weight or he will be even less in love with me than he is now. I know that physical appearance means everything to him."

TRIAL

Kathleen's trial would last over seven weeks. The prosecution would state that she murdered the four children by smothering them in bouts of anger. They would replay a tape of her police station interview and she tried to run out of the courtroom.

Her defense attorneys argued that she did not kill or harm her children. They offered various excuses for the deaths of each of the children, stating it occurred because of Cot Death and with the nearly two-year-old Laura it was a case of myocarditis. She would have numerous friends come to her defense telling the jury of her caring nature. Paramedics and police authorities all described her as appropriately distraught during their visits.

The defense's best argument was that there was no physical evidence that could link Kathleen to murder. Kathleen did not give explicit admissions that she killed the babies.

GUILTY

On May 21st, 2003, Kathleen would be found guilty by the Supreme Court of New South Wales. She would be sentenced to forty years in in prison with a non-parole period of thirty years. On February 17th, 20th the court would reduce her sentence by ten years with a non-parole period of twenty-five years.

Because of the nature of her crimes, Kathleen is in protective custody in order to safeguard her from violence from other inmates. She still writes her foster sister from jail and was upset that her diaries have been made public.

"They are not literal," Kathleen complained. "Definitely not a window to my brain."

"My brain has too much happening," Kathleen would write in one of her more ominous passages. "Unstored and unrecalled memories just waiting. Heaven help the day they surface and recall. That will be the day to lock me up and throw away the key. Something I'm sure will happen one day."

BABY KILLER

The True Story of Amelia Dyer

Chrissy Eubank

Amelia Dyer, considered one of the most prolific serial killers in history, was born around 1837 in Victorian Britain. Her picture on the front cover easily betrays the evil that resided within her heart. Her reign of terror lasted over twenty years, as she is projected to have killed as many as 400 children before finally being caught

She embarked on a thirty year career of killing with eyewitnesses seeing at least six babies entering her house a day. The count of 400 dead is a conservative estimate.

EARLY LIFE

Amelia was the youngest of five children born into the tiny town of Pyle Marsh. She had three older brothers, Thomas, James, and William along with an older sister named Ann. Her father was a shoemaker named Samuel Hobley and her mother was named Sarah Weymouth.

But he didn't come from an impoverished family like so many others during the Victorian Era.

"For the time, she had a pretty good start," said author Allison Rattle. "Her father had a pretty good trade and paid for her to go to church and school which at the time only a quarter of the children her age actually got an education so she was privileged in that respect."

She found entertainment in reading and used to write poetry herself. Amelia's mother Sarah, however, became mentally ill after suffering from typhus fever. Amelia had to suffer through watching her mother's seizures and outbursts, providing care for her until she died in 1848.

"She witnessed her mother basically losing her mind," said Rattle. "And dying a slow, horrific death. I guess being a young girl she may have been called upon to nurse her mother slightly or at least wait upon her."

Psychologists have posited that it was going through this trauma of watching her mother lose her mind, that caused Amelia's own emotional wiring to run askew.

"Amelia would later claim that her mother died as a result of hereditary insanity," said author Allison Vale. "I think though that this isn't true but it's really easy to understand how she could have remembered it that way."

"It was certain to have a massive impact on her and she may have learned a few things about what kind of symptoms might be shown by someone whose losing their mind."

Amelia was sent to live with her aunt in nearby Bristol after her mother's death. She started an apprenticeship with a corset maker and worked there until her father died in 1859. The oldest brother, Thomas, took control of the family shoe business. Two years later, some type of estrangement occurred with her brothers, specifically James and Amelia doesn't appear to have further ties with her family.

In 1861, Amelia moved to Trinity Street, Bristol. She married George Thomas, who at 59 years old was 35 years Amelia's senior. The two lied about their ages on their marriage certificate with George claiming he was 48 years old and Amelia claiming she was 30.

A CAREER IN "HEALTH CARE"

Amelia began training as a nurse after she got married.

"Amelia turned to one of the most arduous professions she could have turned to," Vale said. "Nursing was just starting to change. It was post-Crimean war. Nursing was starting to have a much better profile as a result of Florence Nightingale. But it was still a thankless profession."

"It wasn't a caring profession like it is present day," agreed psychologist Laura Richards. "They train you psychologically to be a lot more robust around dealing with people. So she became quite hardy and emotionless from having been trained through the nursing regime."

Amelia became pregnant at the age of twenty-six before she met a woman named Ellen Dane who came to boarder at her house. Dane was a midwife who told her of a lucrative and shady way to earn money. Amelia would use her own home as a front to provide housing for women who had gotten pregnant out of wedlock. They would them give the babies away for adoption or kill them through malnutrition.

They called it baby farming.

"Amelia could see it was a very easy way to make money," Rattle said. "Although with risks involved obviously although Amelia did have training as a mid-wife as well through her nursing experience so it was certainly something she knew she was capable of doing. That was the beginning of a massive change in Amelia's life."

Dane moved her base of operations to the USA while Amelia took her "business plan" to heart. During this time, unmarried mothers did not have access to any kind of subsidy as the 1834 Poor Law Amendment Act did not oblige the fathers of illegitimate children to pay for their upbringing. These laws, coupled with the stigmatization of single mothers, forced the practice of baby farming.

Amelia discussed business strategies with Dane. She knew the best bet was to insist on being paid upfront with a one-time fee. She refused any type of money for continuous care as she knew that would mean the mother would return to visit.

"The one off premiums were certainly not enough to sustain a child's life for long financially," Vale said. "And the only way that it would be profitable for a baby farmer was to subject a child to persist underfeeding that would at some point bring about the infant's death."

"Abortion was not an option," Judith Knelman said. "So the simplest thing to do was hide, have the baby and get rid of it. Pay somebody to take care of it or pay somebody to get rid of it."

The babies were subsequently left on the premises and seen as "nurse children."

"Illegitimacy was seen as hugely immoral," said author Allison Rattle. "Even orphanages would only accept orphans from families where the parents were married and the father had died. They wouldn't accept a child who was born out of wedlock."

"Dickens did a really good job of describing social conditions in the 1850 and 60s," Knelman added. "Certainly there were a lot of poor people. There were a lot of neglected and abandoned children."

"There was no work," said Alan McCormick of Scotland Yard. "There was no social services. There was no welfare. One in every twelve women was a prostitute. A child being born in normal circumstances only had a fifty percent chance of reaching the age of five. So that's how bad it was."

BABY FARMING

"Baby farming was a business carried out throughout the country," said historian Ken Wells. "If a mother was unable to look after their child, there was an option of sending them out to a baby farmer, also known as fostering, with the understanding that they could visit the child whenever they wanted to."

On the surface they were providing a service to a growing need. They took an unwanted child and gave them to a foster parent. Only those foster parents and caregivers didn't always have the best interests of the infant at heart.

"MOTHER'S FRIEND"

The majority of these "caregivers" resorted to starving out the babies. They sedated crying babies with alcohol or drugs usually using Godfrey's Cordial, also known as 'Mother's Friend'. This syrup was one of the most popular medicines given to infants and children in both the United States and England in the latter years of the 18th and early 19th centuries. The syrup was used as a panacea to everything from colic to jaundice to excessive crying to diarrhea. 'Mother's Friend' was harmful despite its harmless sounding name as it contained one grain of opium for every two ounces. Many infants were poisoned from this syrup which was administered in secret by nurses who wanted to keep babies under their care in a deep state of sleep and thus more manageable.

"A hungry child, a noisy child, is a difficult child to raise," author Allison Vale said. "And something that was chillingly referred to colloquially as 'the Quietness' was an over the counter anti-colic cordial and it did contain liquid opium which was laudanum and in some cases brandy."

"People gave babies laudanum when they were supposed to be giving them food," Klansman said. "Because it dulled the need, or dulled the awareness of the baby that it was hungry. Of course it didn't nourish the baby so eventually a baby that was given that and not given enough food would die."

The babies would die from severe malnutrition but the coroner would record the death as "debility from birth", "lack of breast milk" or "starvation."

There were those guilt-ridden mothers who returned to the baby-farming homes to check on their children but would find their efforts blocked. Most would be too scared or embarrassed to inform the police of any wrongdoing. The police themselves had numerous problems tracking any children that were deemed missing.

"Dead infants," Vale said. "Or abandoned infants were as commonplace in British cities as roadkill today. Babies were found parceled up in railroad stations, under railroad arches."

"It was desperation," McCormick added. "For the vast majority of these ladies."

TO A MANNER BORN

With Dane's departure to the States, Amelia set her sights on taking her place in the baby-farming business. She had just given birth to her own daughter, Ellen, but in 1869 her husband George died.

A widow at age 32 with a baby, Amelia needed a new source of income...

She began taking in pregnant women as she placed ads to nurse and adopt the babies. In return, she required a large one-time fee and clothing for the child. She began meeting with expectant young women, convincing them that she was someone who could be trusted in providing a safe and loving home for their child.

Before she followed through with her plan, however, she put her own child up for adoption and sent her away.

"It was a choice that she made," Vale said. "She had options. She could have worked through. But instead what she does is to farm her own child out and opt for the easy money that she seemed to be able to make."

"As Amelia chose to go into the baby farming business," Rattle said. "She was maybe able to travel around here, there and everywhere adopting babies so it made sense for her daughter to be out of the way."

Three years after her first husband George died, Amelia remarried. His name was William Dyer, a brewers laborer from Bristol. They had two children together, Mary Ann aka Polly and William Samuel.

Amelia eventually left William, however, as the latter lost his job and offered little in the way of finances.

Strapped for cash, Amelia decided to dispense with the heavy cost of letting the babies die through neglect and starvation. So after each child was born she promptly murdered them, thus incurring a windfall of profits.

"Baby farmers used different methods," Klansman said. "Some of which are less palatable than others."

"Quite often she would suffocate babies at birth," Rattle said. "Smothering the baby the moment its head came out, before it turned blue as that would be a sign that it had taken its first breath. (She made) it would look like a stillbirth so the death certificate would all be above board."

When her daughter Polly asked why so many babies came and disappeared, Amelia described herself as the "angel maker."

"I'm sending little children to Jesus," Amelia said. "Because he wanted them far more than their mothers did."

"Cold," Alan McCormick of New Scotland Yard said in describing Amelia. "Those kids meant nothing to her. It was just a means of getting money."

It can be argued, however, that once Amelia got a taste of killing she did it more for the power than the money and greed.

"The actual killing of the child," Holmes said. "Watching the child peacefully to some degree die. It parallels perhaps seeing her mother pass away where she felt an almost God-like power over these children that she had decided were going to go to their maker."

AROUSING SUSPICION

"Amelia was already aware of the fact that this was not going to be about her helping children," forensic psychologist David Holmes said. "This was going to be a fairly cruel and anti-mothering act that would be carried out in order to gain all of this money."

Amelia successfully avoided police involvement until 1879, a good ten years into her murderous ways. A doctor became suspicious about the number of child deaths he had been called in to certify under Amelia's care.

"The inquests were held in Somerset," Vale said. "And they're (the police) pretty certain that the babies have died as a direct result of neglect and opium overdose. But they can't prove it. And interestingly, she gets off with a six months sentence with hard labor."

Without a coroner that was able to rule completely against her, Amelia would have undoubtedly been executed by hanging.

"Its incredibly really," Rattle said. "That she only got six months. And there was one example, we read of a chap who got twelve months for stealing a piece of bacon."

Amelia took the punishment hard, becoming an emotional wreck during her jail stay. She resumed her business, however, as soon as she was released.

"In the long term," Holmes reasoned. "It mostly would have served as a very hard lesson in forensic awareness that she wasn't gonna get caught again. And there was no way she was going to leave any evidence which had been the problem in leading up to her capture."

She was sent to mental hospitals for supposed mental illness and suicidal ideations but these seemed to be well-timed acts. From her experience of working in an asylum, Amelia knew the tricks of the trade in order to make her stay an easy one.

"I don't think Amelia Dyer was insane," said Vale. "I think she was a very bad person who deliberately committed murder for profit."

Amelia had both an alcohol and substance abuse problem, using on a regular basis as she began her killings once again.

"Certainly the drugs would have had an impact on her," Richards said. "On her mental state. Maybe induced this complete detachment from reality."

"A long term laudanum habit," Vale concurred. "Will lead to periods of depression. It can lead to mood swings even when you're not under the influence. I think it also exacerbates any underlying mental health issues."

RETURNING TO BABY FARMING

In 1884, British society took a much harder line against baby farming and any sign of neglect or abuse would be reported.

"She definitely changes her modus operandi at this point (after 1884)," Vale said. "She's beginning to murder these children."

In 1890, Amelia took on the care of the illegitimate baby of a governess. She had begun targeting the babies of the more affluent because of the larger amounts of money involved. The higher up the social class the woman was, however, the more risk was involved as the woman may have means to question and come after Amelia.

"This was a young governess who fell in love with the young master of the house that she worked in and had got pregnant," Rattle said. "She was left on her own and she responds to an advert, gets in touch with Amelia Dyer and moves in with her. Amelia was able to gain the trust of this woman as with many others, so much so that the governess was persuaded to leave her baby in the care of Amelia once it was born."

The governess, however, returned to visit her baby months later and immediately became suspicious that the child she was given was not hers. She stripped the baby to see if a birth mark was present on one of its hips. It wasn't and the governess immediately informed the authorities.

The police, however, could never pin Amelia down.

"She managed to put them off time and time again by sending them on wild goose chases," Rattle said. "She said she had sent them to a couple that moved here...that moved there."

Amelia continued to move from town to town but still found herself being stalked by the governess who wouldn't give up.

"She did feel hounded," Richards said. "I'm sure that would have had an impact on her. She would have felt that pressure."

Amelia then feigned another nervous breakdown and a doctor was brought in. "The birds are telling me to do it! The birds are telling me to do it!" she would cry out, forcing the doctor to send her to an asylum.

"She was a very clever lady," Holmes said. "With the police getting close to her and she needed to lose herself and what better place to go than somewhere like that (a mental asylum)."

Her mental illness continued on unabated as she drank two bottles of laudanum in an attempted suicide. Her long term use of opium, however, allowed her to build up the tolerance necessary to survive.

"Amelia would be drawn to the idea of self-medicating," Holmes said. "Possibly seeing it as a route, a means to ease the situation, make it even easier for her to put up with what she was doing."

"She took it (opium) on a regular basis," Richards said. "She took it almost daily so she was an addict. So that would induce a form of state from her mentally where she would be detached from reality and I think that was part of her coping mechanism to detach from the reality of what she was doing."

After that close call and subsequent hospital release, Amelia resumed baby farming and murder.

"Her mental breakdowns were very short lived," Richards noted. "She would be out of sorts for a period of time that get it all back together again. To me that would say there isn't a mental illness there."

A CLEVER KILLER

She wised up to doing things on the books and decided to stop getting doctors to issue death certificates. Amelia decided to kill and bury the bodies herself. In order to do this, she would have to be a killer on the run as inevitably the mothers would come back seeking to reclaim their children or check on their welfare. Amelia took her family to different cities to escape suspicion as soon as things got too hot. She would use a series of different aliases and rename her businesses.

"Amelia committed what many serial killers do," Holmes explained. "The mistake of accelerating and being over enthusiastic. Either for reasons that she was enjoying the process or quite simply greed was driving her over the edge."

Baby farming began to gain the attention and compassion of the British ruling class, however. They asked why if they had laws for the prevention of the cruelty of animals then why didn't there laws protecting children. With the arrest and hanging of Margaret Waters (another baby farming killer) and the fleeing Dyer, Amelia's colleagues were going downhill fast and perhaps she thought her time was limited.

By 1893, Amelia had another breakdown but was released from the Wells mental asylum. This would be the last time she would be hospitalized. She moved to

Caversham, Berkshire with a woman named Jane "Granny" Smith who didn't know of Amelia's exploits.

"She befriends an old lady named Jane Smith," Vale said. "She's widowed and resigned to spend her last days in the workhouse. Amelia seduces her with stories of rescuing the unwanted infants. Of nursing them. And it's a very, very seductive image. And Jane Smith buys into it, wholesale."

Her daughter Mary Ann aka Polly and her husband Arthur Palmer came along as well.

The group moved to 45 Kensington Road, Reading Berkshire in that same year. Amelia had the perfect front. She coached Jane Smith to call her "mother" in front of prospective clients while Amelia would call her "Granny."

A ruse to project a mother-daughter image and put the guards down of the pregnant young women.

"Jane Smith didn't get the life she was promised at all," Rattle said. "She was treated as no more than a servant really. She was made to look after the children, to clean the house."

Amelia then puts her adoptions into overdrive. The babies come in and out of the house with such rapidity that old lady Jane Smith doesn't even learn their names.

Eyewitnesses later claimed that there were six infants a day coming to and from the house daily.

THE MURDERS CONTINUE

The advertisement in the "Miscellaneous" column of the Bristol Times & Mirror newspaper was poignant.

In January of 1896 a popular barmaid named Evelina Marmon gave birth to a daughter out of wedlock. She named the baby Doris and she sought immediately to have it adopted. She placed an ad in the "Miscellaneous" section of the Bristol Times & Mirror newspaper.

"Wanted, respectable woman to take young child." Marmon intended to go back to work and hoped to eventually reclaim her child.

Evelina was a God-fearing farmer's daughter who left the farm for city life. She found work as a barmaid in the saloon of the Plough Hotel, an old coaching inn. She was buxom with blonde hair and had a vibrant personality. She had plenty of suitors and became pregnant by one of the male patrons who left her deserted.

Evelina knew she could not bring up the baby on her own.

She would have to find a foster home for little Doris - to have her "adopted out", in the language of the time - go back to work and hope in time to be able to reclaim her child.

Next to her own ad was an advertisement that read *"Married couple with no family would adopt healthy child, nice country home. Terms, £10".*

Marmon answered the ad which was addressed to a "Mrs. Harding", an alias of Amelia. A few days later Amelia wrote back, saying *"I should be glad to have a dear little baby girl, one I could bring up and call my own. We are plain, homely people, in fairly good circumstances. I don't want a child for money's sake, but for company and home comfort... Myself and my husband are dearly fond of children. I have no child of my own. A child with me will have a good home and a mother's love. It is just lovely here, heatlhy and pleasant. There is an orchard opposite our front door."*

Evelina was assured that she could visit whenever she wished.

"Rest assured I will do my duty by that dear child. I will be a mother, as far as lies in my power."

"It is just lovely here, healthy and pleasant. There is an orchard opposite our front door."

Evelina tried to negotiate a weekly fee for the care of Doris but Amelia wanted a substantial one-time fee to be paid upfront. Evelina, seemingly with no other choice, agreed to pay the £10, and a week later "Mrs Harding" arrived in Cheltenham.

Evelina was surprised that Amelia aka "Mrs. Harding" was old (59 years) and heavy set (over 210 lbs). She remained reluctant at first but gave in as the elderly woman immediately showed her Doris some affection, covering her with a shawl.

Evelina gave the old lady a cardboard box of clothes she had prepared – nappies, chemises, petticoats, frocks, nightgowns, and a powder box. She also enclosed the money and received a signed receipt from "Mrs.Harding."

She accompanied her baby daughter and her eventual killer to Cheltenham station then on to Gloucester. Evelina stood there crying through the hot steam on the platform as the 5:20 p.m train took her baby away.

When Evelina returned home, she described herself as "a broken woman."

Days later, she received a letter from "Mrs. Harding" offering her assurance that all was well with her daughter. Evelina wrote back but received no replies afterward.

Amelia told Evelina that she would be going to Reading but lied. She traveled to 76 Mayo Road, Willesden, London where her daughter Mary Ann was staying. Amelia then took some white edging tape and wrapped it around the baby's neck, making a strangling knot. The baby did not die immediately.

"I used to like to watch them with the tape around their neck," Amanda said. "But it was soon all over with them."

"The idea of strangling and using the tape may make it seem almost symbolical or bizarre to ourselves," Holmes said. "But in terms of criminal awareness she was aware of the fact that if she tried to suffocate a baby its not always absolutely certain that the baby is dead."

The mother and daughter team wrapped the baby up with a napkin. They kept the clothes that Evelina gave her and hoped to sell it to a pawnbroker. Amelia used some of the money to pay the rent to her landlady and gave the woman a pair of child's boots as a present for her own little girl.

The following day, April 1st of 1896, a young boy named Harry Simmons was taken to the Mayo Road residence. Amelia had no spare white edging tape available and used the tape from Doris' corpse to strangle the year old boy.

The next day both bodies were rolled into a carpet bag, their corpses stacked one on top of the other. Bricks were added inside for additional weight. Amelia headed back toward Reading, taking the bus to Paddington and then the train. She dragged the carpet bag through the streets until she reached the River Thames. She had a secluded spot at Caversham Lock and she forced the carpet bag through the railing and didn't leave until she heard it splash into the waters below.

She didn't know she had a witness as a man passed, hurrying on his way home calling out "Good night."

A SHOCKING DISCOVERY

Ironically, only days before the dumping of the bodies a package was fished out of the Thames by a bargeman. This package was the work of Amelia as she had not weighed it down adequately. It contained the body of a baby girl named Helena Fry. With only a small police force available in Reading, a Constable Anderson made a significant discovery. He found a label from Temple Meads Station, Bristol and he used microscopic analysis of the wrapping paper. He found a faintly legible name. A "Mrs.Thomas" and an address.

The address of Amelia Dyer.

The police immediately placed Amelia's home under surveillance. They did enough research on Amelia and knew that she would "disappear" if she thought she was under suspicion. So they decided they would be better served if they would use a young woman as a decoy to secure a meeting with Amelia and discuss the prospect of using her "adoptive services."

On April 3rd, while Amelia was waiting on the decoy to arrive, she answered the door to a police raid. The smell of decomposing bodies radiated throughout her home but no human remains were found. The police found other evidence, however, such as the white edging tape, telegrams describing adoption arrangements, pawn tickets for children's clothing, receipts for newspaper ads and letters from distraught mothers asking about the welfare of their child.

The police determined that in the few months Amelia had been in Reading at least twenty children had been placed into her care. She had been preparing to move again, this time to the town of Somerset.

Amelia was arrested on April 4th, three days after the murders of Doris Marmon and Harry Simmons. The Thames River was searched and six more bodies were discovered, including Doris and Harry.

Each child had been strangled with the seamstress white tape and Amelia later told police that "was how you could tell it was one of mine."

Eleven days later, Evelina Marmon had been contacted by police as they found her name in items found in Amelia's home. Distraught, she came to identify her daughter's remains.

THE TRIAL OF A KILLER

An inquest was held a month later. Amelia's daughter Mary Ann and her husband Arthur were not charged as there was no direct evidence that they were her accomplices. Arthur was set free because of a confession handwritten by Amelia. She wrote:

Sir will you kindly grant me the favour of presenting this to the magistrates on Saturday the 18th instant I have made this statement out, for I may not have the opportunity then I must relieve my mind I do know and I feel my days are numbered on this earth but I do feel it is an awful thing drawing innocent people into trouble I do know I shal have to answer before my Maker in Heaven for the awful crimes I have committed but as God Almighty is my judge in Heaven a on Hearth neither my daughter Mary Ann Palmer nor her husband Alfred Ernest Palmer I do most solemnly declare neither of them had any thing at all to do with it, they never knew I contemplated doing such a wicked thing until it was to late I am speaking the truth and nothing but the truth as I hope to be forgiven, I myself and I alone must stand before my Maker in Heaven to give an answer for it all witnes my hand

Amelia Dyer.

— April 16, 1896

On May 22nd, 1896, Amelia appeared in court and pleaded guilty to the murder of Doris Marmon. Her family and friends testified that they had their own suspicions about Amelia and spoke of times that she evaded discovery. A man came forth claiming he had seen and spoken to Amelia as she had disposed of two bodies at Caversham Lock proved key to the prosecution.

Amelia used insanity as a defense, offering her stays in mental asylums as proof of her instability. The prosecution, however, argued that her symptoms were well-rehearsed actions to avoid suspicion as both of her hospital stays coincided with times that Amelia felt her murders would be discovered.

The jury took four and a half minutes to find her guilty. Amelia then spent three weeks in her condemned cell, filling five journals with her confessions. A chaplain visited her the night before her execution and asked if she had anything to confess. She offered him her journals, asking "isn't this enough?"

Amelia was then subpoenaed to appear as a witness in her daughter's own trial for murder which was set for a week after her own execution date. The court ruled, however, that Amelia became "legally dead" after she was sentenced and her testimony would be inadmissible.

On the day of her execution, Amelia discovered that the charges against her daughter had been dropped.

On June 10th, 1896, Amelia Dyer was hanged by James Billington at Newgate Prison. Asked on the scaffold if she had anything to say, she said "I have nothing to say."

URBAN LEGEND?

It remains unknown as to why Amelia's daughter Mary Ann aka Polly was never convicted. Her own daughter provided the majority of the testimony that procured the conviction of her mother but nothing is said about her own involvement.

And the baby murders did not stop after Amelia's death.

Two years after her execution, railroad workers inspecting carriages found a parcel tied up with a string inside a siding on the Plymouth express.

Inside was a three-week old baby girl. The infant was shivering and wet...but alive.

A little research showed that the baby was the child of a widow named Jane Hill. Hill had given the baby to a woman named "Mrs. Stewart" for the one time fee of £12.

"The little one would have a good home and a parent's love and care," Mrs. Stewart had written, her prose eerily echoing that of Amelia Dyer. "Mrs. Stewart" had picked up the baby at Plymouth and dumped her on the next train.

The conjecture was that "Mrs. Stewart" was none other than Polly, Amelia's daughter.

BABY KILLER :

THE TRUE STORY OF GENENE JONES

KORI MAYER

Genene Anne Jones was born on July 13th, 1950 in Texas but was given up for adoption. Her adopted parents had three other children. Two were older and one was younger than Genene.

EARLY LIFE

Her adopted parents were Richard and Gladys Jones. Richard, better known as "Dick", a night club and was a gambler. He was a big spender and generous when he was flush. His club was called the Kit Kat Swim Club, the place had a dance floor with a patio and pool outside. His wife Gladys was the disc jockey at the club and the couple lived an extravagant lifestyle. They had a mansion that looked down on San Antonio, would travel often and they would both have pilot licenses .

At the age of ten, however, Genene's father was arrested for stealing the safe of a customer who had been at Jones' club at the time of the robbery. These charges were later dropped.

It could have been due to intimidation on Dick's part. The man was six feet tall, weighed a solid 240 pounds and was bold. He had an aggressive demeanor when needed and his adopted daughter developed the same traits.

His business soon failed, however. The shady Kit Kat Club soon turned into a family themed restaurant which put Dick further into debt. He then sold off the restaurant and earned a living putting up billboards around San Antonio. Genene would later describe helping her father put up the billboards as one of the happier times of her life.

Still, Genene felt as if she suffered from neglect in the adopted home. The parents had paired off the four kids on the basis of age. Genene had an older brother Wiley and an older sister named Lisa. She had a younger brother named Travis who had a learning disability that she doted on and cared for. Nontheless, she felt jealous of all the attention that Lisa would receive. Genene referred to herself as the "black sheep" of the family and took out her frustrations on her classmates at school. She worked in the library at John Marshall and was described as "kind of bossy" by the high school librarian as she would berate other student volunteers who weren't doing their jobs up to her standards. Short and chubby, Genene felt unattractive and began to become known for lying and manipulating people.

"Lying was like talking for her," one of her classmates recalled as Genene would often tell people that she was related to Micky Dolenz, the band member of the Monkees, and that she would routinely have phone conversations with him all the time.

Tragedy would strike in her teens, however, when her younger brother Travis died in a freak accident.

He had put together a pipe bomb which exploded in his face, sending metal shards into his head. Genene took the loss hard, arriving at the funeral with a large flower wreath, crying hysterically, then feinting.

"You wonder when Genene's mind got twisted," forensic psychologist Dina Foster said. "It had to have been early on in her development when somehow, someway she got a surge of power when she was care taking for someone particularly a child. This was probably her brother, Travis. Being a caregiver for him made her feel important. She realized that she could be respected and have people look up to her until it became twisted."

A year later, her father died of cancer at the age of 56 which further devastated Genene. She had yet to graduate high school and wanted to get married. Her adopted mother refused as she Genene's choice of mate, a dropout named James "Jimmy" Harvey Delany Jr as nothing but trouble.

The two would marry, however, and live in a guesthouse near the mansion. Jimmy, however, was only interested in cars and drinking. The two would squabble often until Jimmy decided to join the Navy. With her husband away a basic training, Genene would not remain faithful, going after both single and married men. She had an affair with the newlywed husband of a former high school classmate. Then she began to tell people she had been sexually abused as a child. After four years of marriage, Genene divorced Jimmy as she stated that he had been physically abusive toward her.

Genene would threaten divorce but the two would reconcile.

"She experienced abandonment twice," Foster said. "The first go around was when her mother gave her up for adoption. The second go around was when her brothers and father died back to back. She had lost two loved ones to illnesses and one to a tragic accident. She felt helpless and out of control. But unlike most people, Genene went the criminal route in order to assuage the pain. She had to do things to get the power and control back."

CAREER LIFE & DIVORCE

Genene entered Mim's Beauty School and became a beautician, finding work at the Methodist Hospital beauty parlor. She had her first child, Richard, in 1972 while she and Jimmy were stationed in Georgia. They would move back to San Antonio but by that time the marriage was failing. She filed for divorce in Bexar County, eight months after Richard was born and stated that her husband was "a man of violent and ungovernable temper and passion" while also accusing him of "unconscionable brutality and physical cruelty." She won a court order that forbade her husband from going near both her or baby Richard. Two months later, however, the couple had gotten back together and the judge threw out the divorce suit.

"Clearly they had an on and off again relationship," Foster said. "Jimmy was hapless, wanting to do nothing more than race cars and party. So in some aspects Genene had found her soul mate, a man who needed taking care of."

But on June 3rd, 1974, Genene filed for divorce again and the couple would battle in the court system for three more years. She would file suit against Delany for failure to pay child support and in August of 1976 she won a contempt citation against him. In March of 1977, both consented to drop the legal battle and in July 17 of 1977 Genene's second child, Heather, was born. She later admitted that Heather had been conceived out of wedlock when she and Delany had another brief coming to terms.

Genene would then move back in with her adopted mother who helped with the babies as she began her training at San Antonio Independent School District's School of Vocational Nursing. Genene was a mediocre high school student but she excelled in the program, earning high grades. She aced the licensing exam and got a job at Methodist Hospital.

Genene only lasted eight months, however, getting fired when she made decisions about patient care in which she had no authority as well as being rude to patients. Genene would later claim that she was fired for standing up to a doctor who was being rude to a patient.

"She was a compulsive liar when she was a kid," Foster said. "And the lying continued into her adult life as it turned into full blown denial. She was never at fault for anything. It was always someone else, doctors, nurses, her mother, her husband. She never lived in the land of responsibility."

REIGN OF TERROR BEGINS

Genene then found work at Bexar County Hospital (now known as the University Hospital of San Antonio) where she was assigned to the Pediatric ICU.

It is here where the trouble officially began.

Her first patient had a fatal stomach disease called necrotizing enterocolitis and the boy died after surgery. Genene did not handle it well, crying hysterically. "She just went berserk," Cherylyn Pendergraft said, the RN that was orienting Genene during this time. Genene went so far as to move a stool toward the baby's cubicle and just sat there staring at the body.

Pendergraft felt the gesture odd considering that Genene had barely cared for the child.

Nonetheless, Genene saw herself as an equal to the RN's on duty and worked extra hard to acquire more knowledge than an ordinary LVN.

She worked the graveyard shift upon hire then transferred to the swing shift where she worked f3 p.m to 11 p.m while frequently volunteering for overtime and extra shifts.

Genene soon took on a reputation as the "nurse who cried wolf" to the many resident doctors who were training at the hospital. She would issue warnings about a child's worsening condition to the intern. If the intern did nothing she would then go to the resident doctor. If that physician did nothing then she would go higher up the chain of command and wouldn't stop until her recommendations were addressed.

Despite her eagerness to be perceived as on the same level as a registered nurse, Genene would skip continuation classes on the proper use of pharmaceuticals. In her first year, she was written up on eight separate occasions for giving the wrong dosage.

Genene wouldn't let any reprimands stop her, however, as she soon became the ward bully in the cramped quarters of the pediatric ICU. She would intimidate other nurses with her coarse demeanor, making more than a few transfer out of the unit to get away from her.

Her bullying tactics enabled her to make the unit her own, as she was the foul-mouthed Queen of the ward, bragging about her sexual escapades and making inappropriate remarks.

"Here we see the beginnings of tacit approval," Foster said. "No one at the hospital wants to put themselves on the line to stand up against her. It is an environment where everyone is trying to cover their own ass. No one wants to play snitch even when this woman is saying and doing all of these inappropriate things."

Even more disturbing is that Genene would also predict which baby would die.

During "report", a time in which the nurses would describe the conditions of their patients during the shift change handover to the next nurse, Genene would play the role of the Grim Reaper.

"This patient is really bad," she'd say forewarning the nurse, or even predicting death." This patient isn't going to make it."

By 1981, Genene would always demand to be assigned to the sickest patients. She seemed to enjoy the adrenaline rush of the code blues and would grieve when the child expired. Genene would hold the dead bodies and sing to it, making sure she would be the one to take the corpse to the morgue.

"She had a twisted hero complex," Foster said. "She thought of herself as equal to any RN. Most LVNs defer to the registered nurses out of education and experience. But it was quite the opposite with Genene. When the shit hit the fan she would be the first to come to the rescue. The problem was that she created these situations where she could be seen as the hero. Remember she didn't give them enough medication to kill them outright. She gave the babies just enough of a dose so that they would go into cardiac arrest. She wanted to be seen as the savior to the parents of the children she was killing. She wanted to be seen as the hero of the ward. This need was so deep-seated that she was willing to kill to get that need met. That need to be seen as a hero. That need to be seen as the most compassionate of all."

TOO MANY PATIENTS DYING

Co-workers became concerned that a surprising number of patients under the care of Jones were dying.

"The other nurses became concerned," said Vincent J.M. Dimaio, the chief medical examiner at the time. "That there were increased numbers of cardiopulmonary arrests on the ward. All her victims were children. The most innocent of the population. This would not have happened if the cases had been reported to the medical examiner's office."

Unlike most hospitals, Bexar County didn't lock their medications in a cabinet. When it become apparent that children were dying in the unit from non-fatal illnesses, the hospital dragged its feet in an investigation. There was a two-week period where seven children died in the unit. These deaths occurred only when Genene Jones was on duty and the patients were under her care.

"Astonishing," Foster said. "The tacit approval now extended to the cover up of children being murdered. The hospital administrators put their own public relations and jobs above the lives of children. It is a travesty of justice that no one at the hospital was ever punished for this."

Genene had an ally in the department in the form of Dr. James Robotham, however. Known as "JR", a reference to the ruthless businessman from the TV show Dallas, Robotham was an aggressive doctor throughout his tenure in the ICU. He had no problem dressing down nurses or student doctors who were not up to snuff or did not bend to his will. He had no hiring authority in the hospital but took on a vital role throughout the ICU by placing the patient's care onto his shoulders.

Genene saw a kindred spirit in Robotham and the doctor took a liking to her. There was one occasion in which he needed assistance and chose Genene over another nurse.

"She had been validated," Foster said. "She also wanted to be acknowledged for her nursing talents and finally there was someone who came along and anointed her as someone who was worthy."

"Robotham's Pet" as some of the nurses would later call her, would nonetheless display a macabre interest when a child came in with a fatal illness. Genene would make it clear that she wanted to be on hand when death inevitably came.

Genene would enjoy calling the parents to inform them of their child's death, sharing in their grief over the phone.

"She was Jekyll and Hyde," Foster said. "With the nurses and staff she would be coarse, demanding and condescending. But with the parents of the children she turned into the ultimate caregiver. Soft-spoken, compassionate, and joining them in their pain. She would have the parents believing that she was the most caring person on the face of the earth."

Never mind the fact that she would orchestrate the medical emergency of the child.

"That was her way of getting attention," Dimaio said. "She was a 'big person'. She was a 'big person' when she resuscitated children. When she brought them back from death's door. And the rest of her life, she wasn't anything."

THE KILLINGS MOUNT

A six month old baby named Jose Antonio Flores came into the unit with non-fatal symptoms: fever, vomiting and diarrhea. Unfortunately, he came under the care of Genene.

The baby soon suffered a seizure went into cardiac arrest and died.

Genene grabbed the dead baby and ran out of the department with the staff having to track down the crying LVN. The infant was later blood-tested and the results revealed that there had been an overdose of heparin, an anti-coagulant.

No one had ordered that the drug be administered and now the staff became suspicious.

When questioned about the baby's death, Genene resorted to manipulation and blackmail. She told the staff that she took records on every child that had died there and she knew which doctor had killed them.

Finally, one of the doctors informed the hospital administration what he suspected of Genene Jones. He had found a book in her possession about how to inject heparin through the skin without leaving a mark.

The hospital administrators, however, did not want the bad public relations fall out that would result from being a hospital that had a reputation for infant deaths.

"Say that they expected one (death) a week," Dimaio said. "All of a sudden they were getting three or four or five a week. I don't think there was any doubt that they had a good idea of what she (Genene) was doing."

"The amazing thing here is that even after the incident with the Flores' baby, Genene was allowed to continue working on the ward," Foster said.

Another child came into Genene's unit, this time to recover from open heart surgery. The child made progress but during Genene's shift he died.

"They notice that all of them (the deaths) were on the same shift," Dimaio said. "And all of them involved patients being taken care of by Genene Jones."

More doctors complained and a committee was set up to investigate. Head nurse Pat Belko and James Robotham were in charge on the hospital end but an outside team of investigators came in to look at the problem.

This third party team declined to put the blame on Genene as their findings were inconclusive.

COVERING THEIR ASS

Confident of they were in the clear, the hospital reports no abnormal deaths to the county medical examiner. Still, the hospital knew that Genene Jones was responsible for the deaths.

"She was left on the ward even though they knew what was going on," Dimaio said. "Someone said why don't we just fire her? Then they said well she'll just sue us and they'll be a big scandal. There were more interested in saving their reputation and not being sued then in the life and health of these children."

In order to avoid a public relations debacle, the administration decided to replace the LVNs in the unit with registered nurses. They said they were raising the "training bar" for ICU nurses and that LVNs would no longer be needed.

"So when they adopted that policy they let her go from that unit," Dimaio said. "Let go by the way, with an excellent letter of recommendation. Even though they knew what was going on."

Genene had been suspected in the deaths of over 47 other children, the NYT noted that the administration of Bexar County Medical Center and the University of Texas Medical school had shredded over 9,000 pounds of pharmaceutical records, records that were created during the time when Jones worked there.

By doing this, these administrators effectively destroyed any evidence that would be helpful in convicting Genene Jones of more crimes. The hospital stated that the shredding of documents was "routine" and a "coincidence", but the district attorney was able to intervene when, acting on a tip from an informant, he stopped the hospital from destroying an additional 50,000 pounds of pharmaceutical and medical records. The dean of medicine at Bexar was then cited for contempt of court when it was discovered that she withheld hospital reports from the grand jury.

"This is certainly an indictment of the hospital," Foster said. "If over 47 children were murdered, than there would have to be justice. The irony here is that the hospital administrators are not that far off from Genene Jones' mindset. They lie, deny and keep things in secret. All for the sake of control. All for the sake of being perceived that they are something they are not. Genene wanted to be seen as a hero but was really a killer. The hospital wants good pr at all costs, even childcare's lives. They are scum."

THE MURDERS CONTINUE

After her release from the county hospital and with a letter of recommendation in hand, Jones found work at a pediatric physician's clinic in Kerrville, Texas.

"She ended up here in Kerrville after she left San Antonio because of all these unexplained deaths," district attorney Ron Sutton said. "Genene Jones absolutely despises me because I brought down her little self-constructed impact."

The clinic was a start-up to be run by Dr. Kathleen Holland. She only had budget for an LVN and immediately thought of Genene Jones. She had remembered Genene and had been impressed by her take-charge personality and competence.

Holland contacted the human resource office at the hospital and inquired about the availability of Genene. Holland knew about the strange rumors about Genene but was willing to overlook them as she needed someone who could bring passion to their start up.

Holland didn't know how true those weird rumors were..

"She would create these medical emergencies," District Attorney Ron Sutton said. "That only she would know to handle. Then she would look like this supreme nurse when she would take care of the emergencies that she created."

Holland's revelation began with Petti McClellan brought in her young daughter Chelsea. McClellan said that Chelsea had a "bad cold" and went into the exam room with Dr. Holland. Genene then took the young baby out of Chelsea's arms, stating that she was going to "play" with the baby so that she and the doctor could talk.

"She had an irresistible compulsion," Foster said. "Doesn't matter where she is at, a hospital, a clinic, she has that compulsion. She'll see the opportunity to be a create the scenario for herself and she takes it."

"The protocol for the doctor's office would be the nurse, Genene Jones, would take the baby into a separate room just she and the baby, to perform whatever cursory examination; weight, blood pressure, whatever," Sutton said. "But during the time Genene would have these children by themselves all of a sudden they would become like a rag doll. And then she would scream out 'the baby's not breathing.'"

Moments later, Genene would cry out for help, saying that the baby couldn't breathe.

Doctor Holland immediately jumped into action, seeing that the baby had gone into a seizure. The child would be transported to a hospital and her life was spared.

The McClellan's expressed their gratitude toward Holland and Genene. They thought the world of the duo, believing that they saved the life of their child.

Little did they know that Genene had injected the child with succinylcholine.

Genene had used various methods to kill children under her care. She used injections of digoxin, heparin and later succinylcholine to cause a "code blue" in her patients. She would revive them afterward and receive praise. The succinylcholine she used is a paralytic that causes a temporary paralysis of skeleton muscles which can affect a patient's breathing. When she injected small children with this drug, the victim would suffer from cardiac arrest.

Petti would later return to the clinic months later with Chelsea. She had actually called the clinic to make an appointment for her son Cameron but Holland insisted that she bring Chelsea in so that she could "check on her."

"My daughter wasn't sick," Petti would later say.

Holland later disputes the claim that she asked Petti to bring Chelsea in instead of Cameron.

Unfortunately, Petti would bring Chelsea in and witness Genene administer two shots. The second shot would cause Chelsea to go into a seizure and later die.

"Once she began doing it," Foster said. "She couldn't stop. She became fueled by the adrenaline. The rush she got by sticking the syringe into the baby. The rush she got in waiting for the child to go into cardiac arrest. The the rush she got by watching the child die and comforting it in its death. She even got off on informing the parents of the baby's death. That is how twisted her mind was."

"Her original intent may not have been to kill," Foster said. "She was all about being seen as the hero, the Superwoman who came into save the day. Why she would target the same child coming in for another routine check-up really shows that she was getting careless about her victims. She had gotten away with it for so long that she didn't care. Plus, the compulsion would override whatever logic and forward thinking she had."

Chelsea's death was initially seen as sudden infant death syndrome.

"That's when we talked to the anesthesiologist," Sutton said. "He said that this child looks like it was coming out from the effects of succinylcholine, and we launched our investigation at that point."

"Soon as she got that first shot," Petti McClellan said, "Chelsey immediately starting reacting to it. And I asked her right off the bat, 'what did you do? What did you do? Something's wrong with her.'".

Genene visited Chelsey's grave and seemed genuinely remorseful.

"She was a psychopath with conflicted emotions," Foster said. "On one hand she had this need to kill and be in control of what others thought of her, specifically as a hero. And the other hand, she may have felt remorse when her 'heroic' efforts didn't produce the results she wanted."

Chelsey's mother, Petti, however, was shocked to see Genene at her daughter's grave.

Holland would later find puncture marks in a bottle of succinylcholine in a storage cabinet that only she and Genene had access to. "There were two holes in the lid of this bottle," Sutton said. "One where she had withdrawn and then she attempted to replace it with saline solution."

With the investigators closing in, Genene began to panic. She arrived at the clinic after lunch and complained to Holland that she was feeling ill...She had overdosed on her anti-depressants and began looking lethargic.

Holland immediately called the paramedics and Genene's stomach was pumped. Later upon her release, Texas Ranger Joe Davis interrogated her about the holes in the bottle of succinylcholine. Genene denied involvement, stating that she would be willing take a polygraph test.

The next day, Holland was shocked to see Genene report for work as if nothing had happened. She then informed Genene that her services would no longer be needed. Genene grew enraged and challenged Holland to take a polygraph. She then stormed out of the office.

Genene would later call back to the office and informed Holland's secretary that she had left a letter for the physician in her drawer.

The letter was a one page suicide note that she had written before she had taken the overdose of anti-depressants.

"There isn't anyway to explain to you why things are going to change. Sometimes, as wrong as it may seem, you have to except what life dishes out.

When your older, and I know your tired of hearing that, but you will be able to understand why, why I have to go away. It doesn't mean I don't love you. Please believe that. No amount of money or worldly goods could every buy my love. It is so deep & strong, it will last for all eternity.

Please explain if you can to Heather & Michael how much I love them. It's such a strong love, I can't put it on paper. I know I'm asking a lot, but I really feel your the only one who could do it.

I'm not guilty of murder, & I hope you believe that. But Daddy's way is right. It takes all the pressure off you and the seven people whose life I have altered.

No one can hurt me with my Daddy. He'll straighten this whole thing out & then we'll go home & everything will be alright. No more problems for you, no more nightmares for me.

Please make sure Michael and Heather are not separated. I know how my mother feels about Heather, but I also know how she feels about Michael. If Debbie or you can't take them together, please be sure whoever does are good people. People with lots of love.

Please don't be angry. I'm going with Daddy because I miss him and I want to be with him. He'll take care of both of us.

You'll be fine. Please believe that.

I love you,

Genene

Genene had attempted to frame Holland for the murders but all evidence pointed to her. All said and done, Genene had poisoned at least six children at the clinic. Three of the parents continued to utilize Holland as their pediatrician while three other families sued both Holland and Genene Jones as they believed that Holland knew or should have known about Genene's murderous ways.

The criminal investigation began and Chelsea's body was exhumed, revealing traces of the succinylcholine.

Her exact numbers of victims remain unknown as hospital officials first "misplaced" then destroyed records of her activities to prevent lawsuits after Genene's first conviction.

Genene would go on trial on January 15th, 1984 for the murder of Chelsea and injury to the other children. On February, 15, 1984, Genene was convicted of murder after a three hour deliberation. She was given the maximum sentence of ninety-nine years. In October, she went on trail for injuring Rolando Jones with an injection of heparin. She was sentenced a total of 159 years with the possibility of parole that came up after serving ten years.

In 1985, Gene was sentenced to 99 years in prison for killing fifteen month old Chelsea McClellan.

Later that year, she was sentenced to a term of sixty years in prison for the attempted murder of Rolando Jones with heparin.

"I've had several cases that stand out in my mind," Sutton said. "But this one is particularly heinous because of death to small children.

SERIAL KILLER TO BE RELEASED

Genene Jones is now set to go free because of a legal loophole in the form of She is now scheduled for mandatory release in February 2018 due to a Texas law that prevents prison overcrowding. Genene has been a prisoner who has exhibited "good behavior", becoming eligible for the release.

"Please, please, please, do not let this person walk," Petti McClellan said.

"Genene Jones is probably one of the worst types of serial killers because keep in mind who her victims were," said Andy Kahan, a victim advocate. "Defenseless, voiceless, babies. One of the nation's most diabolical serial killers in our country's history is set to be legally released,"

"I was so angry that it went on for so long," Cherlyn Pendergraft said. "That so many children had to die."

Jones now claims to be sickly and is housed in medical jail unit.

"Am I prepared that she walks?" McClellan asked. "No. Because she's gonna hurt another child. I don't want to hear that she's sick. Or that she's old, she's two years older than I am."

"There is absolutely no reason for Genene Jones to be walking the streets," Foster said. "She has a compulsion that has to be satiated. She needs to be locked up for the rest of her life."

The current District Attorney is looking to re-open old cases against Jones in order to keep her in prison.

MARCIA KELLY

The morning of October 23, 2005, seemed to start much the same way as any other morning in the sleepy town of Cushing, Texas. Marcia Kelly, a 35-year-old mother of three, was wrapping up a grueling night shift at the nearby hospital where she was employed. As the sun began to rise, she made a phone call to her stepfather-in-law, David Bone. Marcia explained to the older man, still drowsy from a sound sleep, that she had been trying to send a "wake-up call" to her husband, James Kelly, with little success. A trucker by profession, James had spent the previous evening "off" deep in routine maintenance of the automobiles that supplied his livelihood – having finally retired at around 2 am, he had requested that his wife rouse him early the next morning via a telephone call in order to get a head start on the upcoming day's tasks. Bone's household stood just a few hundred yards from his stepson's property, so he had no obligations to fulfilling Marcia's request to check on James in person.

Friendly with the family and familiar with the humdrum routine of everyday life in Cushing, Bone suspected nothing amiss when he walked through the door of the Kelly residence. But upon reaching James' bedroom, he suddenly became hesitant. Nothing seemed particularly out of place aside from a cell phone, which lay open on the floor as if it were waiting for somebody to use it. The figure of a man was clearly visible beneath the sheets of the bed, but Bone found its stillness to be unsettling. After a minute or so of not being able to wake up the bed's occupant with the butt end of his walking stick, David mustered up his courage and pulled away the quilt covering up the body. What he found underneath was something truly horrific. The lifeless corpse of James Kelly laid stiff beneath the blankets, surrounded by a pool of blood draining from a single bullet lodged deep into his skull.

Immediately, Bone called 911, though he knew it was far too late for his son to be saved by even the most skilled doctors. Once the ambulances and investigators sounded their sirens and rushed to the scene, it was up to him to notify Marcia as to why her husband would not return her calls. Utterly shocked, she clocked out of work and rushed straight to the crime scene she had once called home. Only upon her arrival would the Kelly family's nightmare be fully realized. Amongst whispers shared between curious neighbors gathering around the flashing lights and barricade tape, the identity of the sole suspect in the brutal murder became crystal clear – Shaina Sepulvado, Marcia's eldest teenage daughter.

* * *

Fourteen years earlier, James and Marcia met eyes for the very first time. Friends often described him as a "good old boy" – the charismatic 19 year old was constantly seeking out adventure, despite the fact that it often landed him in trouble. Although Marcia was only two years his senior, she had already made her way down a much darker path. After dropping out of high school in the ninth grade, she began hanging out with the rowdy crowd of petty criminals. Between the ages of 17 and 21, she had been married (and divorced) twice. The two marriages subsequently produced two healthy daughters. However, motherhood did very little to tame Marcia, who continued to frequent the party circuit filled with drug abuse and drag racing. Concerned with little outside of having a good time, the two soon crossed paths and became instantaneously attracted to one another. On the surface, the feisty girl who wasn't afraid to get down and dirty seemed to be the perfect fit for him. For the next several years, the two casually dated on and off. Neither made fidelity a priority in the relationship; over their first few years together, James had two sons with another woman, while Marcia gave birth to a third daughter by a different man. Ultimately, their non-committal attitudes likely kept their relationship together through the affairs. Regardless of everything that happened, the two had a mutual understanding of one another and always managed to find their way back into each other's arms.

Unfortunately, circumstances finally came about that forced the pair to grow up and leave behind the wild lifestyles of their past. In 1995, James was convicted of violating probation and was promptly sent to prison. Just a few months later, a tragic fire destroyed many of the family's possessions and stole the lives of Marcia's mother and middle daughter, Kaitlyn. Though the eldest and youngest daughters were spared from the flames, the surviving children did not escape unscathed. Shaina, just 6 years old at the time of the incident, fell into a deep depression following the loss. At the height of her grief, the little girl attempted suicide by riding her bicycle straight into the path of an eighteen-wheeler barrelling down the road outside of the family's home. Although she escaped unharmed, Shaina was sent to the hospital for a psychiatric evaluation and remained there for several months to receive treatment. Shaina would never truly recover from the trauma – following the suicide attempt, she became aloof and defiant; "a child that pushed people away," as Marcia described it.

More often than not, these types of unfortunate events split relationships apart at the seams. The opposite held true for Marcia and James. With the time and distance to think about their past decisions, both became incredibly motivated to turn their lives around for the better – together. While James sat behind bars, the two began writing letters to one another in which they'd discuss their plans for the future. After years of fun and games, the two had grown to become each other's support system.

When he was finally released from the county jail, James immediately began saving his money. He eventually invested in a big rig truck, and after many long hours and thousands of miles logged, James began to reap the fruits of his labor. He hired several employees and two more trucks, transforming himself from an independent driver to the head of his own small firm by the time he reached his 30's. While her partner worked behind the wheel, Marcia found the drive to put herself back in school. After studying respiratory therapy, she was able to find steady work in her local hospital. She further capitalized upon her earnings through a self-launched bounce house rental service on the weekends. With a great deal of hard work, the blue-collar couple quickly began to climb the rungs towards a middle-class lifestyle. As their financial pursuits blossomed, so too did their romance. Marcia and her daughters shared a home with James and his sons when the two finally decided to get married. Although she was content with a simple courthouse ceremony after the failed relationships of her past, James insisted they properly proclaim their love in front of family, friends, and God in a traditional chapel wedding. On Valentine's Day 2003, they celebrated much more than their union – the Kelly family used the opportunity to rejoice over the positive changes they had made and the seemingly bright future that lie ahead of them.

From an outsider's perspective, their story sounds like a whimsical, idealistic, all-American fairy tale. Beneath the surface, however, tensions quickly began to boil over and dreams for the future began to dissipate.

One distinctive characteristic that set the Kelly's apart from the average family was their capacity to fight with one another. Whether the adults became quick to anger with the stresses they adopted or one or both of them had a propensity for meanness stitched into their DNA remains a mystery. Regardless of the reasons behind their temper, husband and wife were well known for their volatile screaming matches. Often times, the eager to please James would have to satiate Marcia by purchasing expensive gifts or automobiles. Unfortunately, the fighting branched out beyond the two parents. Shaina, aged 14 at the time of the marriage, was less than ecstatic about the new life she was being forced to lead. With a new stepfather as well as two step brothers living underneath her roof, her behavior shifted from rebellious to completely out of control, and at times, violent. Taking a step out of her mother's handbook, she became involved with the wrong crowd that frequently found themselves in trouble. Naturally, her parents became concerned. Unfortunately, that concern drove a wedge between the newlyweds instead of bringing the two together. Marcia firmly believed that the best solution to deal with her daughter was to allow Shaina the space and freedom to make mistakes – eventually, she'd grow tired of a wild lifestyle and settle down, just as Marcia had done. She didn't question whether her daughter attended school, or where she might disappear to on the weekends.

James saw things much differently. Anxious to be a father figure to his new stepdaughter, he believed that discipline, boundaries, and stern rules were desperately needed to keep Shaina from danger. The discord in the family pushed the teenager towards moving out to a boyfriend's house, adding fuel to the heated arguments between stepdaughter and father. Frequently, Shaina would spit venomous threats concerning her desire to kill James. Meanwhile, Marcia and James would continuously argue over what the right course of action was for their child. The situation finally came to a head when Shaina returned home after the inevitable break up with her live-in boyfriend. Shortly after being forced under her parent's roof, she willfully refused to clean a messy room. What should have been a fleeting tantrum instead escalated into a physical altercation; after assaulting her own mother, authorities arrived and placed Shaina under juvenile probation. Her punishment proved to be not very effective. Rowdy as ever, the teenager soon began dating a 23-year-old sex offender by the name of Dallas Christian. The young lovers eloped in favor of a life of partying and riding without rules, much to the displeasure of James Kelly.

Despite his best intentions, James should have been relieved by the absence of his stepdaughter. She would soon prove to be the person responsible for his untimely demise.

* * *

In the heart of East Texas, just over 600 people call the former railroad town of Cushing their home. As is the case with many of the tiny, close-knit communities scattered throughout rural America, word travels at an incredible speed. Needless to say, word of James Kelly's murder reached a good portion of the townspeople within just a few hours of the event. Though the details surrounding the crime were hazy at best, rumors surrounding Shaina and James' troubled relationship flew out of the lips of neighbors. Although no one wanted to believe that such an atrocity could have happened in Cushing, everyone was able to come to a consensus and agree that Kelly had one (and only one) true enemy in all of Nacogdoches county – his own stepdaughter. It seemed that she was the only one who could have committed the crime so effortlessly. However, close family friend Kevin Dill was among the first to direct his suspicions toward a less likely suspect.

As one would expect from the spouse of a recent murder victim, Marcia was anxious to abandon her shift at Lufkin Memorial Hospital upon receiving the grim news from David Bone. Also typical of a person who has just experienced a devastating emotional blow, Marcia found herself too distraught to drive herself home. Instead, she requested that Kevin Dill pick her up and escort her to the horror that awaited her upon her arrival. As fast as he possibly could, Dill picked up the wife of his best friend. The two proceeded to drive down an empty country road at over 90 miles per hour, only to be stopped by a patrolling sheriff. Sobbing, Marcia hysterically explained the situation to the officer and successfully evaded a speeding ticket. However, shortly before approaching the Kelly household, Dill was startled by Marcia's sudden change in demeanor. Witnesses described her as "flat" and void of emotion. While bystanders wrote her demeanor off as the result of severe shock, Dill was startled by the direct contrast to the display she had put on moments before. After asking if the news of her husband's death was true, Dill recounted another instance of bizarre behavior. Rather than mourn her husband or ask to see the body of the man she supposedly loved, Marcia immediately became concerned with whether the family dogs had been fed breakfast. Amidst questions and concerns from authorities and neighbors alike, she retreated into the house and filled their bowls with food. Though Dill himself was in shock from the sudden death of his friend, he struggled not to attach meaning to Marcia's actions.

Suspicions aside, it immediately became clear that the murder had been intentionally planned out and executed based on a surface investigation. Nothing seemed to be particularly out of place or disheveled inside of the house, and with all of the family's valuables intact, the possibility of a robbery gone wrong was quickly ruled out. In fact, former Nacogdoches county sheriff Thomas Kerss described the scene as "serene". From the available evidence, it seemed as though the murderer strolled through the front door, shot Kelly, and left as if nothing had happened. Marcia firmly denied that anyone, in particular, held a grudge against James when asked about possible enemies. However, the fingers pointed toward Shaina and the men she surrounded herself with were not purely based on conjecture. Aside from the obvious animosity within the family, the group of teenagers were notorious for their erratic and unruly behavior around town fueled by drugs and alcohol. Further backing up the theory was the simple fact that Shaina Sepulvado, Dallas Christian, and Colton Weir (a juvenile who had found himself in and out of trouble with the law over the years) were conspicuously not present among the growing crowd of townspeople clamoring for more information. Certain that the trio must somehow be involved with the crime, police promptly tracked down Christian, Weir, and Sepulvado and arrested them in connection with the grisly murder.

At the initial interrogation, all three maintained their innocence. However, their guilt became apparent as inconsistencies began to take form in each of their stories. The teens claimed to have spent the night shooting guns by the banks of the Shawnee River, a popular hotspot for underage drinking and teenage debauchery. After not getting much out of Sepulvado and Christian, interrogators focused their efforts towards cracking the youngest of the trio, who seemed to be plagued with a guilty conscious. It didn't take much pressure to produce results – on the verge of tears, Colton Weir confessed to being the one to pull the trigger of the rifle that killed James Kelly.

* * *

For Colton, Shaina, and Dallas, partying wasn't so much an undesirable habit as much as it was a way of life. The teens tested positive for cocaine and methamphetamines, which they claimed to have used all day, every day while "riding the roads". On the 23rd of October, the three had been binging on drugs and alcohol and did, in fact, end up drinking down by the river as the night began to wind down. While inebriated, they discussed plans they had made previously to kill James Kelly. They had been talking about the possibility of committing the crime for some time, but had always held off, waiting for a more opportune moment – that is, until that drunken autumn night. Filled with adrenaline and far beyond clear thinking, the three agreed that the time had finally come.They proceeded to drive towards their prey through winding wooded roads, and upon their arrival, ceremoniously fetched gloves and a hunting rifle Weir had borrowed from a friend.

Quietly, Shaina led Colton into the house and directed him toward the room her father slept in. She then returned to the safety of the car, where Dallas Christian waited behind the wheel. Creeping through the darkness, Colton entered the bedroom to find James sleeping soundly after a long day's work on his mechanics. Just 10 feet away from the victim, he lifted his weapon and shot just once. The bullet made impact just above James' cheek, killing him instantly. The blood spattered teen returned to his friends outside, and together they made their way back to the riverbank. After tossing the gun into the water, they proceeded to burn several pieces of incriminating evidence.

The admission didn't come as a surprise to anyone – not only did the details add up to what authorities had found, it was eventually revealed that Colton had confided the murder plot to a number of townspeople ahead of time. Later on, investigators were able to use Colton's account to retrieve the rifle and damaged evidence almost effortlessly. When informed of their friend's confession, both Dallas Christian and Shaina saw the futility in lying about what they had done and dropped the charade of innocence. However, one thing remained uncertain to investigators. While Shaina's motive was crystal clear, it was hard to understand why the two men would get themselves involved in a serious crime against a man they hardly knew.

The answers Colton and Dallas had to offer caught the police completely off guard. Rather than pegging responsibility for the crime on Shaina's charm or ability to manipulate, the two young men instead placed their blame on a different person entirely – Shaina's mother, Marcia.

* * *

"Marcia had a desire to be 18 again," stated Lead District Attorney John Heath in an interview several years after the murder. It was no secret to anyone that the Kelly's marriage was far from picture perfect. However, unbeknownst to many of the residents of Cushing, Marcia had not completely given up her past. She continued to use drugs and alcohol frequently, and while her husband was on the road, she allegedly struck up sexual affairs with the neighbors. It was on these men that she first began toying around with the idea of getting rid of her husband permanently. What began in jest would soon become deadly serious, and after the murder, several men confessed that Marcia had offered them cash rewards for the life of James Kelly. Many refused to be involved outright, and Marcia would move on in search of a better foot soldier. Eventually, she found the pawns she was seeking in the young men her daughter surrounded herself with.

Nacogdoches, Texas was recently recognized as one of the poorest cities in the United States. With the median household income in Cushing falling well below that of Nacogdoches, many of the people in the tiny East Texas town had come to not expect much out of life. Born into unlucky circumstances, the boys Shaina spent her time with came from working class families struggling to get by. Marcia, on the other hand, was beginning to work her way out of generations of financial ruin. Unlike many of Cushing's residents, she was able to promise cash rewards, brand new trucks, and jet skis – luxuries the boys could only dream of. In addition to the monetary incentive, both Colton and Dallas were close to Shaina. Having heard countless stories of his rough, brutish nature, the boys were convinced that James Kelly was a violent, controlling man that deserved to be punished. Between the pleas of mother and daughter, the prospect of murder not only seemed like the morally right thing to do, it also seemed to be advantageous in the long run.

As it turned out, Marcia Kelly's motives for organizing the crime weren't far off from those of the teenagers she masterfully manipulated. The marriage was disintegrating because of the constant arguments and the fundamental disagreements over how to raise their children. Although

Marcia was willing to give up on the marriage, she wasn't willing to give up the financial stability that came with the marriage. Hatred or an escape from a toxic relationship didn't fuel the crime; instead, greed served as the driving force behind the actions. A quick look at Marcia's background and personal finances revealed that she had recently filed a $100,000 life insurance policy on her husband. A funeral director later remarked that she had asked several questions regarding cashing in on the insurance as they made arrangements for James' funeral, striking him as extremely cold and callous. In addition, Marcia was set to inherit nearly all of the assets from her husband's lucrative trucking business. If all went well, she would be wealthy for the rest of her life once her husband took his final breath.

Ever since Marcia's failure to inform the police of the tumultuous relationship her daughter and husband shared, police had been skeptical. When initially confronted about the possibility of her daughter being a culprit in the murder, she claimed that she had written off the threats Shaina had posed as the ranting and raving of any teenage girl. Initially, investigators had simply questioned whether Marcia might be covering for her guilty daughter. However, nobody had considered that she was the mind behind an elaborate murder for hire plot. Evidently, Marcia was confident that the authorities would not catch on to her – so much so that she had already spent hours at the police station of her own volition, claiming to be offering her daughter emotional support throughout her interrogation.

Friends, family, and neighbors were fooled as she played the part of conflicted mother and grieving widow well. Deflecting any suspicion with ease, members of the community offered condolences and helping hands, completely unaware of Marcia's guilt. On the day of James Kelly's viewing, the ceremony was interrupted by officers seeking out Mrs. Kelly. While mourners clad in black surrounded the body of the murder victim, police escorted the surprised Marcia Kelly back to the station for further questioning. She initially cooperated with authorities but quickly grew annoyed by the prospect of missing her husband's funeral. Before she could ask to turn back around to the procession, it was too late. She was presented with a warrant for her arrest and promptly taken into custody. Horrified, she plead for her freedom as she was locked away.

* * *

Nearly a year passed between Marcia's arrest and the beginning of her trial in the summer of 2006. As expected, she claimed her innocence in front of a jury of East Texans, hoping for the utmost sympathy. Unfortunately for her, Colton Weir, Dallas Christian, and several other men opted to take the stand to testify against her. The prosecution proceeded to bring to light the insurance policy and history of violence, cementing Marcia's untrustworthiness as a defendant. The mounting evidence certainly built a convincing case against her; however, none of it was able to conclusively link Marcia to the crime. Luckily, the prosecutors had a secret advantage to bring the case to a close.

The night shift at Lufkin Memorial Hospital was a strong enough alibi to place Marcia far from the scene of the crime on the night of the murder. However, during Colton Weir's confession, he admitted to investigators that Shaina had been in constant communication with Marcia throughout the night of the murder. With that sort of reasonable cause for suspicion, the courts were able to subpoena both mother and daughter's phone records. They revealed that there had in fact been a series of phone calls between the women during the window of time that the murder could have occurred. One call took place just moments after the estimated time of death; Shaina later reminisced that her mother had simply asked, "Is it done?" In addition, Marcia's phone records revealed that she had been in close contact with James leading up to the murder. Prosecutors speculated that these calls were made in order to get an idea of the victim's plans for the night, including when he might be headed for bed. As Marcia collected information regarding her husband's whereabouts and schedule, she would call her daughter in order to conspire how to best strike down James.

Despite all the affirmation against her, one person stood by Marcia's side and rallied for her freedom – her own daughter, Shaina. In her heartfelt testimony, she knowingly took the stand and revealed damning evidence that confirmed her guilt in the murder. Unafraid of taking full responsibility for the crimes she committed, Shaina claimed to the jurors that she had executed her father as a way to end the constant fighting in her household – independent of any goading from Marcia. From there, she went on in detail about her stepfather's alleged abuse over the years. Under oath, she claimed that she had been beaten and molested multiple times throughout the years by the man who so badly wanted to be her father. There may have been truth behind her allegations; even the District Attorney assigned to the case conceded that James was the sort of man "who would probably use the belt from time to time" to discipline his children. Whether there was any truth to the story or not, her testimony ultimately did very little to sway the opinion of the court. Prior to taking the stand, Shaina had never made any mention nor allegations of being abused by members of her family, calling to question her overall credibility. In addition, she adamantly proclaimed her mother's complete innocence despite the implications others had made suggesting otherwise. In retrospect, prosecutor Stephanie Stephens reflected, "You've got to give Shaina a little credit, because when her back was against the wall, she did not drop her mother in the grease. But Marcia Kelly, the moment her back was against the wall, she dropped her daughter in the grease." And indeed, Marcia allowed her daughter to take the fall for her.

Ultimately, Marcia Kelly was convicted capital murder despite her daughter's best efforts to deflect the jury's attention from the facts. Although the state of Texas could have opted for the death penalty, it was eventually decided to be too harsh a punishment to pursue. Instead, she was sentenced to life in prison without possibility of parole. After the sentencing she was taken from the courtroom and transported to the Gatesville, Texas Department of Criminal Justice Mountain View Unit. Kelly was not the only one to receive proper punishment from the justice system for the murder of her husband. In separate trials following Marcia's conviction, Colton Weir and Shaina Sepulvado were likewise found guilty of capital murder and sentenced to life in prison without parole. However, as luck would have it, the Supreme Court found in 2012 that the life without parole sentence applied to crimes committed as a juvenile falls under the category of cruel and unusual punishment. In accordance with the US Constitution, the two can apply for re-sentencing and, with some luck, hope for a life outside of captivity. Dallas Christian ended up with a lighter sentence than his companions – after pleading guilty, he received only 40 years behind bars. Additionally, friends of the murderers Billy Loftin and Gary Batchelor were found guilty of lesser charges, including tampering with crucial evidence.

* * *

Since mother and daughter have been locked away, the story has continued to captivate the local community. Some are haunted by the acts the women committed - others believe the sentencing to be a horrible mistake.

Though nearly a decade has passed since the sentencing, Marcia Kelly remains in the Mountain View Unit to this day. She continues to insist upon her innocence, firmly denying having had any involvement in her husband's death. She has appealed several times to have her ruling overturned. Each attempt has been fruitless, and it's likely that Marcia will spend the rest of her life in a cell. Shaina, on the other hand, has made the most of the situation and even maintains relationships with those roaming the outside world. Through a prison pen pal system, she was able to strike up a romantic relationship with fellow Nacogdoches resident J. Patrick Capps. After some correspondence, the two eventually married.

Capps sincere belief in Shaina's testimony led him to create a web campaign in an attempt to free Marcia. The site he created on her behalf included Marcia's detailed version of events leading up to and following the crime. However, the site has since been taken down. Capps was stopped from publically speaking out on the matter when he was convicted of posting falsified documents online, including a phony notarized statement alleging to overturn the final verdict signed by a state deputy. But Capps' stunt represents just the tip of the iceberg of support both women have received over the years. Guilty verdicts aside, many remain sympathetic to the circumstances mother and daughter have faced. In fact, nearly 1500 people have signed an online petition to free Shaina, believing her abuse allegations to be true and her sentencing to be unfair due to her mental capabilities and youth.

As time has passed, the story has attracted attention far beyond the rural suburbs of East Texas. In 2011, TLC's Prison Diaries featured the case - Snapped, a true crime television series airing on Oxygen followed the story shortly afterward. Later on, Investigation Discovery featured Marcia Kelly and her daughter on two separate programs, Redrum and Fatal Vows. Dozens of articles surrounding the case have been published by local and national news sources, catching the eyes of readers across the United States.

In many ways, Marcia Kelly is a relatable character. Plenty of people struggle through unhappy marriages weighed down with baggage. Tens of thousands of people fight each day to continue putting food on their kitchen tables. The description of Cushing, Texas falls in line with many tiny towns scattered throughout the countryside. What truly sticks out about Marcia is the way that she chose to deal with the frustrations that so many of us face on a daily basis. Because of her choice, Nacogdoches county may never feel quite as safe as it once did. Frightening and fascinating, the fact that's most disturbing of all is that Marcia wasn't a cold blooded psychopath. Instead, she was a calculating individual looking for more than her life in Cushing could offer – a woman with dreams that may fall in line with many of our own.